S0-BNS-151

The Lord Chose... Who???

Henry M. Morse

The Lord Chose... Who???

Cover art
Jews praying in the Synagogue on Yom Kippur
Maurycy Gottlieb 1878,
Tel Aviv Museum of art

This work is in the public domain in the United States, and those countries with a copyright term of life of the author plus 100 years or less.

The text of the New American Standard Bible® may be quoted and/or reprinted up to and inclusive of one thousand (1,000) verses without express written permission of The Lockman Foundation, providing the verses do not amount to a complete book of the Bible nor do the verses quoted account for more than 50% of the total work in which they are quoted.

Scripture quotations taken from the New American Standard Bible®,
Copyright © 1960, 1962, 1963, 1968, 1971, 1972, 1973, 1975, 1977, 1995 by The Lockman Foundation
Used by permission." (www.Lockman.org)

Copyright 2012 by Henry M. Morse, all rights reserved.
www.themessianiccongregation.com
benafuchi@aol.com

ISBN 978-1-4675-4599-0

Dedication

I would like to dedicate this work to the memory of my pastor, Gerald B. Manning, who loved this little Jew boy. He was like a father to me. He prophesied over me and helped me realize the calling in my life. If it wasn't for brother Manning, I would not have become the man I am today. I am thankful for having a man like him in my life. I know what it is to be a man of integrity who loves the Word of the Lord because of his example.

Foreword

There is a dichotomy in the thinking of American Christianity that there are Jews and Gentiles, and the two have little or nothing to do with each other. This book by Rabbi Henry Morse boldly confronts this mistaken view and argues that in G-d's plan of salvation there is a specific role for both "Jew" and "Gentile." Rabbi Henry speaks to the children of Abraham and identifies their role in the Father's plan of redemption. It includes the gracious election of Abram, the making of a covenant people, and the call to take the message of covenant redemption to the nations (Gentiles). Rabbi Henry reminds them of the divinely given responsibility to take the message of the Father's gracious covenant to the world.

Yet, this book is for Gentiles too. The Gentile church, in many ways, has lost its understanding of the biblical roots of faith (theology). Rabbi Henry's book calls Gentiles to understand—and take seriously—the biblical call to covenant relationship modeled and lived out in the children of Abraham, to understand the "Jewish roots" of their faith. Rabbi Henry's unique life history (and personality) makes such a book like this possible—to speak to both the Lord's chosen people, and to Gentiles. With wonderful humor, and intense seriousness, this book helps to proclaim biblical faith and redemption that guides and shapes a commitment to Yeshua.

Philip N LaFountain, ThD
Associate Professor of Theology
Eastern Nazarene College

Acknowledgements

First and foremost, before I thank anyone, I would like to praise and thank the Lord for putting this work on my heart. It sounds cliché, but I really am a blessed man. I have had a chance to be involved in some very significant areas of ministry. I have travelled all over the world in service to the Lord. Now I get to write a book. Who am I that these wonderful opportunities should be opened up to me? It doesn't get much better than this. Thank you, Lord, for allowing me to be used in this way.

I would also like to express my appreciation to Cherri, my beautiful wife of 36 years. I would not be able to do what I do in the ministry without your support and help. You are my friend, partner, and the apple of my eye. You are an amazing wife, mother, grandmother, and nurse. Thank you, dear, for putting up with me all these years—only 36 more to go!

To my dear sister Lee and brother Lincoln, thanks for sticking with us all these years as partners in the ministry. Your faithful friendship and support has been more valuable than the finest gold. Thanks also for your help in editing this work.

Bob and Kris, you are truly the finest friends and coworkers a Rabbi could have. I could not lead our congregation without you.

Aaharon, thanks for all the editing work. Yu reely maid me luuk edumacated. Wat wood I hav dun wit outcha help?

Michele, your finishing touches on this work made it worth reading. I am indebted to you for the countless hours you spent pouring over the book and catching all the booboos.

Windel, your patience and care for me as a youth was an example of true sainthood. You never let me get away. I will always love and value your friendship. You were the best youth Pastor a kid could have asked for.

Introduction

Of the writing of books there seems be to no end. So you might ask: Why write another one? There are a number of reasons why one writes a book: monetary gain, recognition, the need to communicate a burden, or exercising one's literary and scholastic prowess. Some reasons are nobler than others. The one thing that we do not need, however, is another religious book full of spiritual and religious jargon and verbiage like, "A book that expounds on the concepts of the Christological propitiation for our sins, so that we might understand the profound salvific work that has been wrought for us through the substitution of the Lamb." You get my point.

This is why I feel the need to write. I find that writing helps me to become sounder in my understanding of Biblical concepts and ideas. Writing helps me to understand them properly, in their original context, to both know my subject matter better and also to be able to communicate it clearly to others. Second, I feel that many mainstream religious writers have largely ignored the Biblical subject matter that I would like to cover here. Third, I want to discuss deep spiritual foundational truths in a language that the layman can understand, while not insulting their intellect. People need to be intellectually satisfied and challenged.

In this book the reader will not learn everything there is to know about the Word of G-d; it is only intended to be an introduction to critical Biblical principles that I hope and pray one will go on to investigate in more detail.

My goal is to communicate the simple idea that the Lord created/chose the Jewish people for the blessing of the world. It is critical for anyone who calls himself or herself a believer in the Messiah to understand the role of the Jewish people in order for them to have a healthy, theological perspective. If the truth of the Gospel message is to be fully realized, then this can only happen when it is understood in light of its history, culture, language, and idioms. It is a Jewish message. It was given to the Jews first. It was spoken mostly in the Hebrew language. It was played out historically in the land of Israel.

The western mind thinks with a very Greco-Roman world view. Why would anyone consider that the world view of the Middle East would be the same as that of the Greco-Roman world? Therefore, we must understand this message as a Jewish one to see the original intent of the authors.

This is why I wrote this book, not to mention that I found great joy in this project. I have also realized a great benefit in that I grew more in love with Yeshua (Jesus)—the Messiah of Israel and the world. I pray that this little book will do the same for you.

One more thing I would like to mention. It seems to me that it would be good for every believer to do the same and write their own book. Whether or not you desire publication, this kind of a project would be a benefit to all who take this challenge.

The Author
Messianic Rabbi Henry M. Morse BA, ADD, ADHD, OCD, ETC, ETC, ETC.

Prologue

Since the beginning of "Christianity" there has been a rift between the roots of the Jewish faith and the "Christian" faith. It seems as if those who claim to be believers in the man named Yeshua (Jesus) have done all they can to separate themselves from the idea that this man was a Jew; but we must be mindful that all he said and did was from a Jewish perspective.

This historical rift has made it available to perceive them as two diametrically opposed belief systems. Jewish people believe that Yeshua (Jesus) is the Messiah for the "Christians" and that their Messiah is yet to come.

This is where the problem starts. Very few people of faith really understand that if Yeshua is not the Messiah to the Jews first, He cannot be the Messiah to anyone. There is only one Messiah promised by the Lord.

He was promised first to the Jews so that the Gentiles would also be reconciled to the Lord by this Promised One. Until those who call themselves "Christians" fully understand that their faith is a Jewish one, they will always be teaching a Gospel message that is polluted in some way, shape, or form by paganism.

The Gospel message must be a Jewish one for it to be true to the original intent of the Lord.

Table of Contents

Chapter 1
Abraham: A Nice Jewish Boy

Our goal is to understand the original intent of the authors of the Bible. In order to get the full picture, information must be given systematically and in proper sequence. That means we must start from the beginning to see the message that the Lord is trying to communicate in its context. If we study in this way, then I believe we will see the Lord's real intent in His actions. So, let's start from the beginning, shall we?

In Genesis 12:1 we see the Lord's promise given to Abram because of his faithfulness. The promise is not only to Abram, but it is also to his son and his future progeny. This is seen as the initial call by the Lord to choose a distinct people for Himself. From Abram, soon to be Abraham, came the nation of Israel— the chosen people. We see something curious about this call. The benefit is not exclusively for the seed of Abraham; it is also for the rest of the world.

> Now the LORD said to Abram, "Go forth from your country, and from your relatives, and from your father's house, to the land which I will show you; and I will make you a great nation, and I will bless you, and make your name great; and so you shall be a blessing; and I will bless those who bless you, and the one who curses you I will curse. **And in you all the families of the earth will be blessed.**"

It's not like Abram was moving from Yonkers to Brooklyn. He couldn't just give everyone a call to let them know he got there safely. The Lord was asking him to leave the security of his entire community and give up his entire way of life for something unfamiliar. He was now to venture into the total unknown. This move was beyond extreme. Abram heard the Word of the Lord and responded in faith, and that faith was manifested into action. This move was for the benefit of everyone, "...*all the families of the earth*."

Why would the G-d of Abram be concerned with the rest of the world? My contention here is that, right from the beginning, the Lord's intent in creating Israel is clearly seen in that He made them for the benefit of the whole world.

Who were these people, and why was it important to create them? Were they to be a nation, an ethnic group, or a religion? When we read Genesis17:1-16, we again see something rather curious and distinct about their beginning.

Now when Abram was ninety-nine years old, the LORD appeared to Abram and said to him,
"I am G-d Almighty; walk before Me, and be blameless.
I will establish My covenant between Me and you,
    And I will multiply you **exceedingly**."
Abram fell on his face, and G-d talked with him, saying,
    "As for Me, behold, My covenant is with you,
And you will be the father of a multitude of nations.
    No longer shall your name be called Abram,
    But your name shall be Abraham;
For I will make you the father of a multitude of nations.
    I will make you exceedingly fruitful, and I will make nations of you, and kings will come forth from you. I will establish My covenant between Me and you and your descendants after you throughout their generations for an everlasting covenant, to be G-d to you and to your descendants after you. I will give to you and to your descendants after you, the land of your sojournings, all the land of Canaan, for an everlasting possession; and I will be their G-d."
    G-d said further to Abraham, "Now as for you, you shall keep My covenant, you and your descendants after you throughout their generations. This is My covenant, which you shall keep, between Me and you and your descendants after you: every male among you shall be circumcised. And you shall be circumcised in the flesh of your foreskin, and it shall be the sign of the covenant between Me and you. And every male among you who is eight days old shall be cir-

cumcised throughout your generations, a servant who is born in the
house or who is bought with money from any foreigner, who is not
of your descendants. A servant who is born in your house or who is
bought with your money shall surely be circumcised; thus shall My
covenant be in your flesh for an everlasting covenant. But an uncircumcised male who is not circumcised in the flesh of his foreskin,
that person shall be cut off from his people; he has broken My covenant."

Then G-d said to Abraham, "As for Sarai your wife, you shall
not call her name Sarai, but Sarah shall be her name. I will bless her,
and indeed I will give you a son by her. Then I will bless her, and she
shall be a mother of nations; kings of peoples will come from her."

In this section of Scripture, the Lord establishes the covenant
with Abram through the ritual of circumcision, the Brit Milah.
This was not only for Abram, but for all of his sons who were
eight days old; and not just his sons, but anyone in his household.
Why would the Lord do something like that to His chosen ones?
It seems so barbaric. What we see in these passages is that the
Lord had already promised that He would be the G-d of Abram
and his seed. So what does the Lord do here? He marks him in
his organ of regeneration to remind Abram that He is not his G-d
alone, but He is also the G-d of his seed. Abram will never forget
this, because the mark is always with him.

And you shall be circumcised in the flesh of your foreskin, and it
shall be the sign of the covenant between Me and you. (Genesis
17:11)

The Lord not only made this covenant available to Abram
and his seed, but to anyone who wished to avail himself of it.

Genesis 17:12-14 And every male among you who is eight days old
shall be circumcised throughout your generations, a servant who is
born in the house or who is bought with money from any foreigner,
who is not of your descendants. A servant who is born in your house
or who is bought with your money shall surely be circumcised; thus
shall My covenant be in your flesh for an everlasting covenant. But
an uncircumcised male who is not circumcised in the flesh of his

foreskin, that person shall be cut off from his people; he has broken
My covenant.

So how do we answer the question, "Who are they?" The answer simply is: "they" are a family, and this family is open to all who desire to join either by birth or adoption. Their familial status is a very important concept that must be grasped in order for us to understand the heart of the Gospel. Remember this— we will come back to it later.

We have to be aware of the fact that Abram was not what we think of as Jewish, or an Israeli. He was from Ur of the Chaldeans.

> Genesis 11:31 Terah took Abram his son, and Lot the son of Haran,
> his grandson, and Sarai his daughter-in-law, his son Abram's wife;
> and they went out together from Ur of the Chaldeans in order to
> enter the land of Canaan; and they went as far as Haran, and settled
> there.

This would put him in the area of modern Iraq. He was a Semite, from the line of Shem. His father, Terah, was not even a G-d-fearer.

> Joshua 24:2 Joshua said to all the people, "Thus says the LORD, the
> G-d of Israel, 'From ancient times your fathers lived beyond the River, **namely, Terah, the father of Abraham and the father of Nahor, and they served other gods.**'"

[Midrash Bereishit Rabbah 38:13 (an ancient sixth century CE Jewish commentary on Genesis,) provides for us some information about Abraham's family. The Midrash tells us that Abraham's father, Terah, not only worshipped other gods but also that he was an idol maker. One time when Terah had to travel, he left Abraham in charge of the shop. When customers would come in wanting to purchase idols, Abraham would ask them how old they were. People would answer 50, 60, etc. To which Abraham would respond, "Isn't it pathetic that a man of 60 wants to bow down to a one-day-old idol?" At this the customers would hesitate, feel ashamed, and leave.]

So, just who are these Jews?

There were no such people known as Jews in that point in time. The Lord did not *choose* the Jews, as we understand the concept. He **created** the Jews from a people that were not. Remember, we read above in Genesis 12:2that G-d said, "And I will **make** you a great nation."

> Deuteronomy 7:7 The LORD did not set His love on you nor choose you because you were more in number than any of the peoples, for you were the fewest of all peoples.

They were the fewest of all people because, until then, they existed only in the mind and foreknowledge of the Lord. The people followed the template of their ancestor. In the beginning there was only one, Abram (exalted father), who would later be named Abraham (father of a multitude).

This is what the Lord does. He brings into existence things which were once not in existence, as He brought all of creation into existence of out of nothing, through nothing other than His spoken word.

> Genesis 1:1 In the beginning G-d created the heavens and the earth. The earth was formless and void, and darkness was over the surface of the deep, and the Spirit of G-d was moving over the surface of the waters. Then **G-d said, "Let there be light"**; and there was light.

> Isaiah 45:12 It is I who made the earth, and created man upon it. I stretched out the heavens with My hands and I ordained all their host.

> Isaiah 45:18 For thus says the LORD, who created the heavens (He is the G-d who formed the earth and made it, He established it *and*

did not create it a waste place, *but* formed it to be inhabited), "I am the LORD, and there is none else."

The Lord did not create the world for the benefit of the Jewish people; He created the Jewish people for the benefit of the world.

So what would that benefit be? Let's try and understand it by summarizing the process.

1. The Lord creates mankind to love, and with whom to have intimate fellowship. (Genesis 1 and 2)
2. He gives them only a few requirements to fulfill. (Genesis 2:16-17)
3. Adam and Eve sinned, separating all mankind from their intimate relationship with G-d. (Genesis 3:15-19).
4. The Lord promised there would be a restoration for all mankind through the woman's seed. (Genesis 3:15)
5. The world continued to fall far away from the knowledge of the Lord (Genesis 6:5-8.)
6. The Lord chose a man, Abram, who would listen to His voice. (Genesis 12:1-4)
7. From that man, the Lord created a people who would be dedicated to the purpose of making the knowledge of G-d and serving Him foremost in their lives. (Genesis 12:2; Deuteronomy 4:5-9)
8. Abraham received G-d's promises by faith. (Genesis 15:6; Galatians 3:6-9)
9. The people's knowledge of the Lord was not meant to be restricted to themselves; it was to be shared with the world. (Isaiah 42:6.)

In the next section we will examine the way that the Lord used these people to bring about that benefit to the world.

Chapter 2:
What Do the Gentiles Have to Do With the Jews?

This whole plan was established by the Lord to restore the whole world back to Him. This theme is supported throughout the entire Bible. It is like a thread on which G-d hangs His Word, and it runs throughout the whole of the Scriptures, from beginning to end.

Here is a list of just a few of those scriptures. We can see very clearly, by the repetition of this theme throughout the Bible, that it is not out of context or just an isolated idea. This shows the Lord's intention, as he spoke to the Prophets throughout the centuries with this repeated theme. I have provided the scripture addresses and a brief description of the verses. Please read them yourself. You will find that each of these scriptures has to do with G-d's dealings with the Gentiles. You will also see that, in most of them, the Lord desires to use Israel to deliver this message. In these passages we see the Lord reaching out to the whole world, not just Israel. He wants to recognize them and be recognized by them. You might just say that, for a Jewish book, G-d seems to be a little too preoccupied with the Gentiles. As much as this topic is addressed in G-d's Word, we can see that it is not just a peripheral issue. It is a major theme that should not be dismissed, as it has been in the past by both Jewish and Gentile theologians. The Lord always wanted to reach the Gentile peoples through the nation of Israel.

Take note of the fact that when the word "nations" is used in the Biblical text, most of the time it is the word "goyim" in Hebrew. This is the word we translate as "Gentiles." Often this word is used in a very negative light in contemporary Jewish conversation. But in the Scriptures, it is not so.

Genesis
12:3, 22:18, and 27:4
All the nations of the world will be blessed.

Exodus
20:10 and 23:12;
Deuteronomy 5:12-14
Sojourners are to enter into the Sabbath rest.

Numbers
15:14-16   One law for you and the alien sojourner.

Isaiah
2:2   All the nations will stream to the mountain of the Lord.
9:2   The people walking in darkness have seen a great light.
11:9   The earth will be full of the knowledge of the Lord.
12:4   G-d has done great things; let this be known to all.
19:19-25   The Lord will make himself known to the Egyptians.
42:5-8   A light for the nations.
43:9-12   You are my witnesses; I am G-d.
45:22   Turn to me and be saved all you ends of the earth.
49:6   I have given thee for a light to the Gentiles.
49:22   I will beckon to the Gentiles.
55:4-5   I will call a nation that does not know me.
56:1-8   My house shall be called a house of prayer for all nations.

Isaiah
60:3   The Gentiles shall come to your light.
65:1-3   I am sought of them that asked not of me.
66:18-19   Declare my glory among the Gentiles.
66:20-21   I will take some of them for priests and Levites.

Psalm
9:11   Proclaim among the nations what He has done.
22:27   All the ends of the earth shall turn to the Lord.

46:10	I will be exalted among the nations.
66:4	All the earth shall worship thee.
86:9	All the nations will come and worship you.
96:3-10	Declare His glory among the nations.
98:3	All ends of the earth have seen the salvation of the Lord.
108:3	Sing praises with the nations.

Jeremiah

| 1:1 | I ordained thee a prophet unto the nations. |

Hosea

| 2:23 | G-d will say to them which were not His people, "you are my people." |

Ezekiel

| 6:20-22 | They kept the Passover, the children of Israel, and all that sought the Lord of Israel. |

What we see in these passages is that the Lord is a G-d of inclusion. Admittedly, the children of Israel were not to intermingle with the nations. They were to keep themselves separate. They were not to intermarry, nor even to eat with the heathen, as we see in Ezra 10:10-11:

> Then Ezra the priest stood up and said to them, "You have been unfaithful and have married foreign wives adding to the guilt of Israel. Now, therefore, make confession to the LORD G-d of your fathers and do His will; and separate yourselves from the peoples of the land and from the foreign wives."

But that did not mean that the heathen, if they repented, were excluded from intermingling with them. The Lord wanted Israel to be a light to the nations, (Or La Goyim). They could not be that light unless they opened up to let them in.

Even the Passover festival is meant to show the inclusive nature of the Lord, as He instructs Israel:

> Exodus 12:19 Seven days there shall be no leaven found in your houses; for whoever eats what is leavened, that person shall be cut

off from the congregation of Israel, **whether he is an alien or a native of the land.**

The alien (non-Israelite) was welcomed into the commonwealth of Israel, if he kept the Lord's commandments and if he served the Lord G-d of Israel. All were welcome. I see this not just as a concession by G-d to let a few stragglers in, but as the Lord's clear and full intention.

The Lord reiterates this later in the passage when He says in Exodus 12:47-49:

> All the congregation of Israel is to celebrate this. But if a stranger sojourns with you, and celebrates the Passover to the LORD, let all his males be circumcised, and then let him come near to celebrate it; **and he shall be like a native of the land.** But no uncircumcised person may eat of it. The same law shall apply to the native as to the stranger who sojourns among you.

Right from the beginning of Israel's nationhood, the Lord declared His desire to reach the whole world. This was in order that He might have a relationship with all humankind. The entire book of Jonah is dedicated to the theme of reaching the Gentile Ninevites with the Lord's message of salvation through belief in Him. We read at the end of the book, His justification for sending Jonah:

> Jonah 4:10-11 Then the LORD said, "You had compassion on the plant for which you did not work and which you did not cause to grow, which came up overnight and perished overnight. Should I not have compassion on Nineveh, the great city in which there are more than 120,000 persons who do not know the difference between their right and left hand, as well as many animals?"

It doesn't get any more specific than in Isaiah 56:3-7:

> Let not the foreigner who has joined himself to the LORD say, "The LORD will surely separate me from His people." Nor let the eunuch say, "Behold, I am a dry tree." For thus says the LORD, "To the eu-

nuchs who keep My Sabbaths, and choose what pleases Me, and hold
fast My covenant, to them I will give in My house and within My
walls a memorial, and a name better than that of sons and daughters;
I will give them an everlasting name which will not be cut off. Also
the foreigners who join themselves to the LORD, to minister to Him,
and to love the name of the LORD, to be His servants, everyone
who keeps from profaning the Sabbath and holds fast My covenant;
even those I will bring to My holy mountain and make them joyful in
My house of prayer. Their burnt offerings and their sacrifices will be
acceptable on My altar; for My house will be called a house of prayer
for all the peoples."

Traditional Rabbis throughout history, including our contemporary times, have contended that Yeshua could not have been,
and cannot be the Messiah, because he did not bring about the
time when "the lion will lay down with the lamb" (Is. 11:6). The
Rabbis say that when the Messiah comes, men will beat their
swords into plowshares and their spears into pruning hooks, and
Israel will be restored to its fullness[1]. I concur that there are
prophesies speaking of this worldwide peace that the coming of
the Messiah is to bring about.

Isaiah 2:1-4 The word which Isaiah the son of Amoz saw concerning
Judah and Jerusalem: Now it will come about that in the last days, the
mountain of the house of the LORD will be established as the chief
of the mountains, and will be raised above the hills; and all the nations will stream to it. And many peoples will come and say, "Come,
let us go up to the mountain of the LORD, to the house of the G-d
of Jacob; that He may teach us concerning His ways and that we may
walk in His paths." For the law will go forth from Zion and the word
of the LORD from Jerusalem. And He will judge between the na-

[1] **Raphael Patai's work, *The Messiah Texts* on pages 322-327** "King Messiah will arise in the future and will

*The Lord will return your captivity and have compassion upon thee, and will return and gather thee from all the
peoples whiter the Lord thy God hath scattered thee. If any of thine that are dispersed be in the uttermost parts of
heaven, from thence will the Lord thy God will bring thee into the land which thy fathers possessed, and thou shalt
possess it (Deut. 30:3-5)"*

tions, and will render decisions for many peoples; *and they will hammer their* **swords into plowshares and their spears into pruning hooks. Nation will not lift up sword against nation, and never again will they learn war.**

Micah 4:1-3 And it will come about **in the last days** that the mountain of the house of the LORD will be established as the chief of the mountains. It will be raised above the hills, and the peoples will stream to it. Many nations will come and say, **"Come and let us go up to the mountain of the LORD, and to the house of the G-d of Jacob, that He may teach us about His ways and that we may walk in His paths." For from Zion will go forth the law, even the Word of the LORD from Jerusalem. And He will judge between many peoples and render decisions for mighty, distant nations. Then they will hammer their swords into plowshares and their spears into pruning hooks; nation will not lift up sword against nation, and never again will they train for war.**

We notice that these scriptures are speaking about events that happen specifically in the last days of the world's history. As we have pointed out above, a plethora of prophecies exists speaking about the fact that when the Jewish Messiah comes, he will bring the knowledge of the G-d of Israel to the entire world. This is exactly what happened when Yeshua came to earth.

We now have to ask the question: before Yeshua came, what did the pagans think concerning the G-d of Israel? Yeshua's coming was the single event in history that opened up access to the G-d of Israel for the entire world. If He was not the Messiah, then he was an awfully good imposter. Here are some quotes from the Greco-Roman world that show the sentiment of their philosophers and historians concerning the Nation of Israel and its Lord.

Publius (or Gaius) Cornelius Tacitus, 56 A.D. to 117 A.D., was a Roman historian who wrote about the Jews in his *Histories*, Book V. Tacitus wrote about the exclusive worship of the Jews,

"...the Jews have purely mental conceptions of Deity, as one in essence. They call those profane who make representations of G-d in human shape out of perishable materials. They believe that Being to be supreme and eternal, neither capable of representation, nor of decay. They therefore do not allow any images to stand in their cities, much less in their temples." Tacitus further explains the self-imposed social segregation of the Jewish people, *"...they regard the rest of mankind with all the hatred of enemies. They sit apart at meals, they sleep apart....they abstain from intercourse with foreign women....circumcision was adopted by them as a mark of difference from other men. Those who come over to their religion adopt the practice, and have this lesson first instilled into them: to despise all gods, to disown their country, and set at naught parents, children, and brethren."*

Another writer, Dio Cassius, a Roman historian of the second century, reflects on the established Jewish monotheism in the Roman Empire, *"They are distinguished from the rest of mankind in practically every detail of life, and especially by the fact that they do not honor any of the usual gods, but show extreme reverence for one particular divinity. They never had any statue of him even in Jerusalem itself, but believing him to be unnamable and invisible; they worship him in the most extravagant fashion on earth."*

As we see from the statement above, Jewish worship was reviled by the Roman world. They did not want to know about the G-d of Israel. They deemed Jews to be barbarians.

We now have to ask: Is the predominant Biblical theme for the coming of the Messiah that all nations will beat their swords into plowshares? Or is it that the Gentiles, who reviled the G-d of Israel, will gain a desire to know Him and His Messiah? Are those two events to happen simultaneously or separately? If Gentiles come to know the true Lord of the universe, are they coerced into faith by impending judgment, or are they to come as a result of a loving relationship with G-d? Deuteronomy 4:5-8 says,

> See, I have taught you statutes and judgments just as the LORD my G-d commanded me, that you should do thus in the land where you are entering to possess it. So keep and do them, **for that is your wisdom and your understanding in the sight of the peoples who will hear all these statutes and say, "Surely this great nation is a wise and understanding people. For what great nation is there that has a G-d so near to it as is the LORD our G-d whenever we call on Him? Or what great nation is there that has statutes and judgments as righteous as this whole law which I am setting before you today?""**

As I read this passage, it seems to indicate that Israel was to provoke the nations to jealousy because of the relationship they had with their Lord. In order for this to happen, Israel must live a life that provokes others to jealousy. This provocation could produce fruit only if the Gentiles exercise their free will to choose and align themselves with Israel and their Lord. They were not to replace Israel as G-d's people but to come alongside them. This could not happen only as a result of the "Last Days" kingdom coming to this earth. The Gentiles needed to live out their ungodly lives first, so that they could see the testimony of Israel. Israel needed an opportunity to live out their relationship with their Lord, so that His prophetic Word might be fulfilled through their lives. The fulfillment must not be limited only to the last days. The Messiah had to come before this worldwide peace was established in order for the Gentiles to have a chance to come to the Lord through him. There can be peace in the world only when the Lord first lives in the hearts of men. When this happens, then the Messiah can come again to openly reveal G-d's presence in the world, but only after all men have had a chance to serve him. When we take into consideration all the scriptures that call Gentiles to the service of the one true G-d, worldwide peace cannot be the predominant theme of the Messiah's coming. The Gentiles' recognition of the G-d of Israel is, by far, the more articulated of the two themes. Thus, the Rabbis' argument that Yeshua could not be Messiah because there is no peace is moot.

> Isaiah. 42:6 I am the LORD, I have called you in righteousness, I will also hold you by the hand and watch over you, and **I will appoint you as a covenant to the people, as a light to the nations.**

Chapter 3:
An "Alright" Kind of Gentile

Many biblical characters stand out for their faith and accomplishments before the Lord. But there are few who shine like Caleb. You know Caleb, from the team of Joshua and Caleb, mentioned in Numbers 13:30. He believed the Lord could bring them into the land when everyone else disbelieved the Lord's ability and promise to do this. "And Caleb stilled the people before Moses, and said, '**Let us go up at once, and possess it; for we are well able to overcome it.**'"

Joshua and Caleb were the only two men from the generation of the wilderness who entered the Promised Land. Very few people know this, but Caleb was a certifiable Gentile. You might ask: How is this possible? The Scripture tells us he was the son of Jephuna the Kenezzite. The Kenezzites were to be dispossessed from Canaan, the land that the children of Israel were promised by the Lord in Genesis 15:18-21:

> In the same day the LORD made a covenant with Abram, saying, "*Unto thy seed have I given this land,* **from the river of Egypt unto the great river, the river Euphrates: The Kenites, and the Kenizzites,** and the Kadmonites, and the Hittites, and the Perizzites, and the Rephaim, and the Amorites, and the Canaanites, and the Girgashites, and the Jebusites."

We see these two men entering the Promised Land together as an example of Jewish-Gentile relationships, according to the heart of the Lord. This Jew and Gentile entered into the land together, a generation after the Exodus, foreshadowing the one new man, Jew and Gentile, restored back to his Creator, as we read about in Ephesians 2. (Joshua 14:6 tells us who this "one new man" is, as well as Numbers 14:24, 13:6, 26:65, and 34:19)

In Joshua 14:7-14, this very same Caleb stands before his fellow spy, Joshua, and gives a brief synopsis of his faithful history. He is now ready to receive the inheritance that was promised to him by Moses, which Joshua did give him. We read his words as follows:

> "I was forty years old when Moses the servant of the LORD sent me from Kadesh-Barnea to spy out the land, and I brought word back to him as *it was* in my heart. Nevertheless my brethren who went up with me made the heart of the people melt with fear; but I followed the LORD my G-d fully. So Moses swore on that day, saying, 'Surely the land on which your foot has trodden will be an inheritance to you and to your children forever, because you have followed the LORD my G-d fully.' Now behold, the LORD has let me live, just as He spoke, these forty-five years, from the time that the LORD spoke this word to Moses, when Israel walked in the wilderness; and now behold, I am eighty-five years old today. I am still as strong today as I was in the day Moses sent me; as my strength was then, so my strength is now, for war and for going out and coming in. Now then, give me this hill country about which the LORD spoke on that day, for you heard on that day that Anakim *were* there, with great fortified cities; perhaps the LORD will be with me, and I will drive them out as the LORD has spoken." So Joshua blessed him and gave Hebron to Caleb the son of Jephunneh for an inheritance. Therefore, Hebron became the inheritance of Caleb the son of Jephunneh the Kenizzite until this day, because he followed the LORD G-d of Israel fully.

Boy, those Gentiles have really come a long way!

In the last chapter of the book of Isaiah, we see one of the most remarkable, but possibly one of the most neglected passages in the Bible.

> Isaiah 66:18 "For I know their works and their thoughts; the time is coming to gather all nations and tongues. And they shall come and see My glory. I will set a sign among them and will send survivors from them to the nations: Tarshish, Put, Lud, Meshech, Tubal and Javan, to the distant coastlands that have neither heard My fame nor

seen My glory. And they will declare My glory among the nations. Then they shall bring all your brethren from all the nations as a grain offering to the LORD, on horses, in chariots, in litters, on mules and on camels, to My holy mountain Jerusalem," says the LORD, "just as the sons of Israel bring their grain offering in a clean vessel to the house of the LORD. I will also take some of them for priests and for Levites," says the LORD. "For just as the new heavens and the new earth which I make will endure before Me," declares the LORD, "so your offspring and your name will endure. And it shall be from new moon to new moon and from Sabbath to Sabbath, all mankind will come to bow down before Me," says the LORD.

If I understand this passage correctly, it seems that these events will take place during the millennial reign of the Messiah.

The Lord is going to gather the nations to come and see His glory. He will send out the survivors from the battle of Armageddon to declare His glory to those nations. They will bring back their brethren from those nations to Mount Zion in Jerusalem. Then He will take some of those who were from the nations and choose them for the service of priests and Levites. Remember, the word "nations" in English is the word "Goyim" in Hebrew, also translated as 'Gentiles", i.e. anyone who is not Jewish.

The only way to describe what I see here in this passage is stunning. This Jewish prophet is clearly seeing into the future, that when the Messiah reigns, His authority and kingdom will be extended beyond Israel into the whole world. He will at that time restore the world back to the Lord, and all men will be one in His Kingdom, as He will take from the Gentiles some to serve as Priests and Levites. Then in verse 23 He declares that: **"All mankind will come and bow down before Me," says the Lord.**

It is at that time when the verses of 1 Peter 2:9-10 will be fully realized:

> But you are **a chosen race**, a royal **priesthood, a holy nation, a people for G-d"s own possession**, so that you may proclaim the excellencies of Him who has called you out of darkness into His marvelous light; for you once were **not a people**, but now you are **the people of G-d**; you had **not received mercy**, but now you **have received mercy.**

So we must conclude from just this brief study, that the plan of the Lord always was, and continues to be, to reconcile the world (the Gentiles) back unto Himself. He chose/created the Jewish people for that purpose. As we read earlier in the Deuteronomy 4:5-8 passage, the Lord wanted the world to envy the nation of Israel because of their relationship with Him. He wants us to submit ourselves to Him of our own free will. The problem is that Israel forgot their job description and abdicated their role as the light to the nations. Even in the Talmud Rav Helbo said: "Proselytes are as hard for Israel [to endure] as scabs" (Yevamot 47b). Ouch! Not only did they forget their calling, they turned it over to the Gentiles/Christians, and the Gentiles polluted it. Instead of being grateful for the mercy that was extended to them, the Gentiles persecuted the very people who were the original messengers. Everybody messed up. If this doesn't sound like one twisted plot, then nothing does. It was always Satan's desire to destroy the Lord's plan of salvation for the world. He knew that the way to do this was to attack it from the root. If he could separate the original branches from the root then he would have a chance to undermine the Lord. This is called replacement theology. We will examine this in more detail later on.

To sum it up, these questions must be posed: Is Yeshua the Messiah for the Jew? Is He only the Messiah for the Gentile? The answer is this: If He is not the Messiah for the Jew, He cannot be the Messiah for the Gentile. There is only one Messiah; the One who was promised for the entire world, but He first came to the Jews, for the Jews, through the Jews; "...for salvation is of the Jews." (John 4:22).

There was never an option of a Messiah for the Jews and a separate Messiah for the Gentiles. Again, I reiterate that if Yeshua is not the Messiah for the Jews, then He can't be anyone's Messiah. But because Jews and Gentiles do not know this, they end up separating Christianity from its Jewish roots, and causing a mentality to flourish that Judaism and Christianity are two distinctly separate theologies. If Yeshua is not the Messiah, then it is incumbent upon the Jews to preach this to the Gentiles, in order to fulfill their role as a light to the nations, just like Jonah. By allowing the Gentiles to believe in a false Messiah without contest would amount to total abdication and failure of their G-d-given responsibility to be His tools on this earth.

Chapter 4:
That Man, Rav Shaul (the Apostle Paul), Really Knew His Stuff.

Shaul's understanding of the Scripture from its Jewish root is just astounding. This is not without foundation, as He says of himself in Philippians 3:4-11:

> ... although I myself might have confidence even in the flesh. If any-one else has a mind to put confidence in the flesh, I far more, cir-cumcised the eighth day, of the nation of Israel, of the tribe of Benjamin, a Hebrew of Hebrews; as to the Law, a Pharisee; as to zeal, a persecutor of the church; as to the righteousness which is in the Law, found blameless. But whatever things were gain to me, those things I have counted as loss for the sake of Mashiach. More than that, I count all things to be loss in view of the surpassing value of knowing Mashiach Yeshua my Lord, for whom I have suffered the loss of all things, and count them but rubbish so that I may gain Ma-shiach, and may be found in Him, not having a righteousness of my own derived from the Law, but that which is through faith in Mashi-ach, the righteousness which comes from G-d on the basis of faith, that I may know Him and the power of His resurrection and the fel-lowship of His sufferings, being conformed to His death; in order that I may attain to the resurrection from the dead.

Another much-neglected passage in the history of the "Church" is Romans 11. This passage sums up the plan of the Lord in a magnificent way, such that only Rav Shaul (the Apostle Paul) was able to do. Rav Shaul was able to make the connection from the Tanach (First Covenant law/instruction) to the grace of the Brit Chadashah (New Covenant) without skipping a beat. He saw the natural theological bridge because he knew G-d's Word so well. So when he came to faith in Yeshua, it was not a prob-lematic choice for him, because from his study of the Tanach, he already understood that the grace of G-d extended to the Gentiles. It made so much sense to him, that he wrote two thirds of the New Covenant writings about this issue so that we also could see it. In the Brit Chadashah (New Covenant), we not only see the Gospels and other letters (epistles), but we see Rav Shaul interpreting the Tanach for us, as it was revealed to him by Yeshua, the Messiah, Himself.

> Galatians 1:11-16 For I would have you know, brethren, that the gospel which was preached by me is not according to man. For I neither received it from man, nor was I taught it, but I received it through a revelation of Yeshua ha Mashiach. For you have heard of my former manner of life in Judaism, how I used to persecute the church of G-d beyond measure and tried to destroy it; and I was advancing in Judaism beyond many of my contemporaries among my countrymen, being more extremely zealous for my ancestral traditions. But when G-d, who had set me apart even from my mother's womb and called me through His grace, was pleased to reveal His Son in me so that I might preach Him among the Gentiles, I did not immediately consult with flesh and blood.

Rav Shaul knew why the Lord chose the Jewish people, and he was ready, willing, and able to teach us why. This is clearly expounded upon in the Romans 11 chapter that we will look at in a few pages.

The Natural Branches

We want to be very careful to keep things in context, so we will start in Chapter 9.

Romans 9, 10 and 11 are some of the most neglected passages in G-d's Word by the "Church." I am sure that this has to do with the fact that these passages are quite clear in their presentation of who Israel is in relationship to the Gospel. It is very hard to refute these passages when they are dealt with in their proper context. These verses show us that the Lord is not done with Israel. He has not cast them aside, as some teach. He will be faithful to them because of His promises, and He will always be true to His Word.

Unfortunately, this short work is not able to deal with the amount of extensive exegesis needed to fully work through these passages. These verses could truly be the subject of entire books on their own. I will attempt to bring light to these passages as much as is possible in the allotted space.

Romans 9

In Romans 9:1-5, Rav Shaul declares his desire for the salvation of his people; so much so, that he is willing, if it were possible, to be cut off from G-d for their sake. He also acknowledges in verse 5 that it is from these people that the Messiah comes.

> I am telling the truth in Mashiach, I am not lying, my conscience testifies with me in the Holy Spirit, that I have great sorrow and unceasing grief in my heart. For I could wish that I myself were accursed, separated from Mashiach for the sake of my brethren, my kinsmen according to the flesh, who are Israelites, to whom belongs the adoption as sons, and the glory and the covenants and the giving of the Law and the temple service and the promises, whose are the fathers, and from whom is the Mashiach according to the flesh, who is over all, G-d blessed forever. Amen.

In verses 6-29, Rav Shaul concentrates on the sovereignty and foreknowledge of G-d, as it relates to the natural-born children of Abraham, as well as the spiritual children of Abraham.

> But it is not as though the Word of G-d hath come to nought. For they are not all Israel that are of Israel: neither, because they are Abraham's seed are they all children: but, in Isaac shall thy seed be

called. That is, it is not the children of the flesh that are children of
G-d; but the children of the promise are reckoned for a seed.

Although Rav Shaul differentiates between the two groups,
he never puts one above the other in a preferential sense, as some
suggest. Nor does he substitute one for the other. What he does
reveal is the eternal plan of the Lord to reach out to the Gentiles,
as His intent was from the days of His covenant with Abraham.

Shaul uses the analogy of Abraham, who had another son
named Ishmael. Ishmael was still his seed, but he was not a son
of the promise. The promise was fulfilled through Isaac. Now he
extends this argument to make the point that, just as Ishmael was
not a son of the promise in the flesh, some who are of Israel are
not sons of the promise in the Spirit. This does not contradict the
Word of the Lord because Shaul will point out that this was
G-d's plan all along.

In verses 14 through 16 Shaul makes it clear that the people
He is extending mercy to are the Gentiles, because they have now
been brought in as Abraham's seed in the Spirit. This is not to
replace the natural seed though.

> What shall we say then? Is there unrighteousness with G-d? G-d for-
> bid! For He saith to Moses, "I will have mercy on whom I have mer-
> cy, and I will have compassion on whom I have compassion." So
> then it is not of him that willeth, nor of him that runneth, but of G-d
> that hath mercy.

Verses 22-24 specifically state that it is the Gentiles who are
the recipients of G-d's mercy because He extends to them mercy
that they do not deserve, even though it was always His intent.

> What if G-d, willing to show his wrath, and to make his power
> known, endured with much longsuffering vessels of wrath fitted unto
> destruction: And that he might make known the riches of his glory
> upon vessels of mercy, which he afore prepared unto glory, *even* us,

whom he also called, not from the Jews only, but also from the Gentiles?

This is the mystery of G-d's foreknowledge and our free will working together, to bring about His good and perfect will. No surprises here, because G-d made this known from the start, as Rav Shaul knew, and so magnificently communicated later on in chapters 10 and 11; verses 25 and 26 are very clear that He is talking about the Gentiles:

> As he saith also in Hosea, "I will call that my people, which was not my people; and her beloved, that was not beloved. And it shall be, that in the place where it was said unto them, 'Ye are not my people,' there shall they be called sons of the living G-d."

In verse 27, he then picks up the subject with reference to the remnant of Jews who would come to him as he references Isaiah:

> And Isaiah crieth concerning Israel, if the number of the children of Israel be as the sand of the sea, it is the remnant that shall be saved.

In verses 30-33 He again emphasizes that it is the Gentiles who are the beneficiaries of salvation because of the stumbling of the Jewish people:

> What shall we say then? That the Gentiles, who followed not after righteousness, attained to righteousness, even the righteousness which is of faith: But Israel, following after a law of righteousness, did not arrive at **that** law. Wherefore? Because **they sought it** not by faith, but as it were by works. They stumbled at the stone of stumbling; even as it is written, "Behold, I lay in Zion a stone of stumbling and a rock of offence: And he that believeth on him shall not be put to shame."

Rav Shaul does this to set up the next two chapters, 10 and 11. In these chapters he lays out both the job description and failures of the Jews and Gentiles.

Romans 10

In Chapter 10:1 Rav Shaul deals a little more specifically with the issue of Israel's rejection of the Messiah. But again, he starts the chapter with his desire for Israel's salvation. This is because in Romans 1:16 he states that the Gospel is to the Jew first. This is not a statement of preferential treatment. It is simply the logical plan that the Lord put into action for the redemption of the world. How could he bring the Gospel to the Gentiles first when they had no introduction to the concept of a Messiah? Neither did they know of the prophecies that spoke of His coming. The Gospel is to the Jew first sequentially, but not preferentially.

In verses 2-11 Rav Shaul shows the difference between the righteousness obtained by the law, and the righteousness obtained by faith—specifically, faith in Yeshua, (verses 9-11).

Verses 12 and 13 Shaul again emphasizes that all men are saved in the very same manner—by calling upon His name in faith. In verses 14-20 he now sets up his introduction for the specific role of Israel in this plan of salvation now extended out to the rest of the world. How will the world receive this appointed Messiah without a trained messenger? Unfortunately, the ones appointed for this task have abdicated from their work. The ones who were the targets for reception are now obligated with the task of provoking the Jew to jealousy. This is so they would return and fulfill their G-d-appointed role and be the light to the Gentiles.

Chapter 11

Finally, we come to the "pièce de résistance" (the great masterpiece) of these three chapters. In Chapter 11:1-5, Shaul reiterates that, in spite of Israel's rejection of G-d's Messiah and His plan to save the Gentiles through them, there is no reason for thinking that He has rejected Israel, because everything that occurs was in His foreknowledge. So, he preserved for Himself a remnant from the seed of Abraham. They were preserved by His grace, and they are to whom He would extend His grace. This issue of foreknowledge and free will is one that would seem to make no sense to mortal men. This is true, for I certainly don't understand it. But I am convinced that this is what makes G-d who He is. He is above logic, supra-logical, not illogical.

Verses 6-10 cannot be understood without fully appreciating the nature of G-d's foreknowledge in cooperation with man's free will. Shaul starts out by making sure we are convinced that salvation is obtained only through grace. Israel didn't receive the very thing it sought after—the grace that was promised by the coming of the Messiah. The ones who did receive it were the chosen, or elect of G-d. These are those who came out from the combination of believing Jews and Gentiles, who were called the "one new man" of Ephesians 2. They don't replace Israel; they come alongside Israel. Remember that they were the ones who fulfilled the very purpose of the Gospel, for the purpose of furthering the redemption of the Gentiles of which we spoke in the last chapter. The rest were hard-hearted. The problem starts because of the misidentification of who the elect are; and if the rest were hard-hearted, does that mean they lost their ability to exercise their free will?

Rav Shaul answers these questions very effectively in verses 11-15:

I say then, they did not stumble so as to fall, did they? May it never be! But by their transgression salvation has come to the Gentiles, to make them jealous. Now if their transgression is riches for the world and their failure is riches for the Gentiles, how much more will their fulfillment be! But I am speaking to you who are Gentiles. Inasmuch then as I am an apostle of Gentiles, I magnify my ministry, if somehow I might move to jealousy my fellow countrymen and save some of them. For if their rejection is the reconciliation of the world, what will their acceptance be but life from the dead?

Israel didn't stumble for the sake of her complete rejection, but her fall had a purpose. It was for the redemption of the world. This was made possible because of G-d's foreknowledge. He knew what Israel would do, and in spite of that knowledge, He was still able to give them complete free will.

This quality of G-d might seem to be illogical to some, but as I said above, what kind of a G-d would He be if He was trapped by the constraints of His creation? This is a good example of His supra-logical nature.

This text shows us that Rav Shaul understood the Lord as always having a desire and plan to save both Jew and Gentile, and He used this desire and plan to show that He can make decisions based upon His foreknowledge, in conjunction with our free will, to accomplish His redemption of the world.

In verses 16-24 he now addresses the issue of how the Gentiles should respond to this plan of G-d's. In verse 16, Rav Shaul sets up some foundational concepts that the Gentiles always need to be mindful of—the original dough and root are holy. That makes the lump that was pinched off and the branch that was broken off holy also. The lump and the branches that he is talking about are the children of Israel:

If the first piece of dough is holy, the lump is also; and if the root is holy, the branches are too.

In verses 17-23, he warns the Gentiles, who were branches from the wild olive tree, to be careful to not boast about the fact that some of the natural branches were broken off, so that these wild olive branches might be grafted in:

> But if some of the branches were broken off, and you, being a wild olive, were grafted in among them and became partaker with them of the rich root of the olive tree, do not be arrogant toward the branches; but if you are arrogant, remember that it is not you who supports the root, but the root supports you. You will say then, "Branches were broken off so that I might be grafted in." Quite right, they were broken off for their unbelief, but you stand by your faith. Do not be conceited, but fear; for if G-d did not spare the natural branches, He will not spare you, either. Behold then the kindness and severity of G-d; to those who fell, severity, but to you, G-d's kindness, if you continue in His kindness; otherwise you also will be cut off. And they also, if they do not continue in their unbelief, will be grafted in, for G-d is able to graft them in again.

The natural branches (Israel) were broken off because of unbelief, and as a result, the wild olive branches (the Gentiles) now had room to be grafted into the cultivated tree. This should produce an attitude of gratitude from the Gentiles, not one of boasting and arrogance. It is the Lord's desire to graft back into the tree the natural branches, but only if they do not continue in their unbelief. As for the Gentiles, they are still obligated to continue and persevere in faith.

This plan seems to express a kind of circular logic. It all gets back to the same concept. The Lord created the Jews to reach the Gentiles. The Jews fell away from their call, and the Gentiles were invited in to provoke the Jews back by making them jealous. This is definitely not the plan I would have thought up, but when we look at it retrospectively, it works just fine. Verses 24-36 sum it all up and explain this circular logic very nicely:

> For I do not want you, brethren, to be uninformed of this mystery—
> so that you will not be wise in your own estimation—that a partial
> hardening has happened to Israel until the fullness of the Gentiles
> has come in; and so all Israel will be saved; just as it is written...
> From the standpoint of the gospel they are enemies for your sake,
> but from the standpoint of G-d"s choice they are beloved for the sake
> of the fathers; for the gifts and the calling of G-d are irrevocable. For
> just as you once were disobedient to G-d, but now have been shown
> mercy because of their disobedience, so these also now have been
> disobedient, that because of the mercy shown to you they also may
> now be shown mercy. For G-d has shut up all in disobedience so that
> He may show mercy to all. Oh, the depth of the riches both of the
> wisdom and knowledge of G-d! How unsearchable are His judgments
> and unfathomable His ways! For who has known the mind of the
> Lord, or who became His counselor? Or who has first given to Him
> that it might be paid back to him again? For from Him and through
> Him and to Him are all things. To Him be the glory forever. Amen.

In verse 25 he describes it as a mystery. As I said, it is supra-
logical. Israel's heart was hardened so that the Gentiles might
come in. Verses 26-27 say that all of Israel will be saved, but only
after the Gentiles' predomination of the Gospel is complete. This
does not mean that every Jew that has ever lived will be saved.
This refers to those who come to faith after the "time of the
Gentiles" is through. This has to be the case, because salvation is
still by grace through faith. As Rav Shaul says in Ephesians 2:8:

> For by grace you have been saved through faith; and that not of
> yourselves, it is the gift of G-d; not as a result of works, so that no
> one may boast.

Israel still has to receive the Messiah and His sacrifice, just
like everyone else. Romans 11:28-32 silences anyone who tries to
use the Brit Chadashah (New Testament) as a tool to promote
their agenda of anti-Semitism. Rav Shaul clearly shows that we
are all enemies of the Gospel apart from the Lord's mercy,
whether we are Jews or Gentiles.

34

Verses 33-36 sum it all up by again stressing that it is all a mystery of G-d's eternal nature, as Isaiah 40:13 says: **"Who has directed the Spirit of the LORD, or as His counselor has informed Him?"** In all G-d's ways, He is just and gracious, in that He gives mercy to all of us; he gives us loving-kindness that we don't deserve, and spares us from our deserved judgment. It is all because of the plan that G-d shared with us from the beginning in the Tanach (Old Testament). This plan was to create a people for Himself who would preserve the knowledge of who He was until the time would come when the world would be ready to receive Him, by their own free will, back into their life as Creator, Father, Savior, Priest, and King.

We grow in faith by study of the Word of G-d. The Word was given for the purpose of our benefit. If G-d's Word is studied in its original history, culture, language, and idiomatic language, it puts meat on the bones of our theology. Once we take it out of its Jewish Biblical context, we have to find another filter through which to interpret its words. Everything in G-d's Word was given to show the prophetic display of the coming of the Messiah; every holiday, passage, and prophecy. They were very specific. The Lord called them appointed times and seasons, "moadim" (Lev 23:4). They were given to point to the Messiah. They also functioned as mnemonics so that we could rehearse and remember who Yeshua was, in the past, present, and future.

If we decide to change this in any way, what prevents us from changing all of it? Once we allow our faith to be pulled from its roots in any way, we are then opening up the door for the entire plan to look different, as we see again in Romans 11:17-21:

But if some of the branches were broken off, and you, being a wild olive, were grafted in among them and became partaker with them of the rich root of the olive tree, do not be arrogant toward the branches; but if you are arrogant, remember that it is not you who supports the root, but the root supports you. You will say then, "Branches were broken off so that I might be grafted in." Quite right, they were broken off for their unbelief, but you stand by your faith. Do not be conceited, but fear; for if G-d did not spare the natural branches, He will not spare you, either.

Where do we draw the line? When is "contextualizing the Gospel" actually changing the Word of G-d? If the Gentile is now grafted into the family of G-d and has become a spiritual seed of Abraham, then why would he want to change the family dynamics or structure to fit his desires or non-Jewish perceptions? Why not come into the family as it is if it functions just fine? How is this new way better than the original one? Again, we must remember that we grow in our faith through the very specific detailed presentation of the Gospel in its biblically Jewish context. If you ignore this, there are many holes to fill. If your faith is not based on the Word of G-d, it is based on what you feel at that time. If it is solely based on feelings, we can join any cult we like. For many of them base their interpretation of Scripture on their subjective feelings.

The illustration below is not original to me. The only problem is that I can't remember where I saw it first. So if you know its origin, please inform me so I can give credit where it is due. This is what the body of believers is supposed to look like. Unfortunately, the "Church" today is quite different than the illustration in its practice.

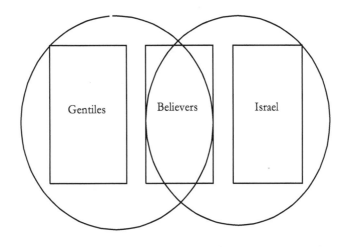

Jew and Gentile are to function as one in Messiah. Separate in their identity and job description, but one in every other way, just as a man and woman are simultaneously one in relationship, yet separate in body.

The problem is that the "Church" has an identity crisis. They don't know who they are in Messiah or what they are supposed to be. This is why there are so many different denominations with their varying degrees of doctrines.

The Scripture says in Galatians 3:28, "There is neither Jew nor Greek, there is neither slave nor free man, there is neither male nor female; for you are all one in Mashiach Yeshua." This might be true in Messiah, but don't tell me my wife is not a female. I'm sure you get the point.

Chapter 5:
Does the Church or Anyone Else Now Replace Israel?

Replacement theology is an attempt by Satan to usurp Israel from its place, hence, throwing the Messiah from His place. This is an age-old plot concocted by Satan to keep the world from receiving the salvation that was promised. If he can throw Israel from its place, then he can replace it with a substitute that can't produce salvation. He then makes G-d a liar. There are some in the "Church" who believe and teach that the promises given to Israel are now null and void because of Israel's rejection of their Messiah. These promises are now assumed to be owned by the "Church." We have partly dealt with that issue in the last chapter, but we will now discuss it in more detail.

One of the problems with this theology is that in order for the Messiah to come again, Israel must be a nation in its Biblical homeland, promised to Abraham (read Ezekiel 36 and 37, Jeremiah 30 and 31, Daniel 9:24-27).

If the Yeshua-believing Gentiles, who call themselves the "Church, replace the people of Israel, then it is their obligation to move back to the land of Israel, so that they might be in place to fulfill the end-time prophecies. If they can't do that, then they can't be Israel. Satan knows this, and that is why he has tried for centuries to usurp Israel from its place. He has not only tried this with some in the "Church," he has used false religions in the same manner.

One of the worst forms of replacement theology is Islam. They not only try to make Israel illegitimate, they go as far as to say that they were never the chosen ones, because it was through Ishmael, not Isaac, that the Lord's promise of salvation to the world was extended. They define which portions of the Bible are inspired and which are not. They plagiarize small portions of the Word of G-d—primarily names and places—and then put the Biblical characters and places into Muslim theology.

The Qur'anic Narration[2]

The name of Ishmael does not appear in the Qur'anic text. However, the Qur'anic narration gives the sequence of events that happened before and after the sacrificial offering. These chronological events very precisely testify that Isaac was born after the event.

Abraham pleads for a Son:

"O my Lord! Grant me a righteous (son)!" So we gave him the good news of a boy ready to suffer and forbear. Then when (the son) reached (the age of) serious work with him he said: "O my son! I see in a vision that I offer thee in sacrifice: now see what is thy view!" (The son) said: "O my father! Do as thou art commanded: thou will find me if Allah so wills, one practicing Patience and Constancy!" So when they had both submitted their wills (to Allah) and He had laid Him prostrate on his forehead (for sacrifice). (Qur'an 37:100/103)

---

2 From the website www.mostmerciful.com

The good news for the birth of Isaac—a righteous prophet—comes much later; hence, "they had both submitted." The above verse refers to Abraham and his eldest son, Ishmael. (See also Qur'an 37:111/113.)

The above verses clearly indicate that the incident of Supreme Sacrifice happened before the birth of Isaac, and Ishmael was the "only Son" of Abraham, as mentioned in the Book of Genesis 22:2, 12, and16."

The question I must ask is this: Why is the Bible quoted as an authority in some places, and in other places it is ignored? How did Islam become the final word for what is, or is not, to be accepted as Biblical authority? If I remember correctly—and I do—the Septuagint text was started by the third century BCE and was completed by 132 BCE. The Septuagint, or simply "LXX," is an Ancient Greek translation of the Hebrew Bible. The story is quite a bit different than the Quran's narration, which was completed sometime around 653 AD.

Islam represents itself as the revelation of G-d on this earth. There is no room for anyone else to have an opinion. They believe that their religion was the original intent of the Lord from the beginning. They claim that all of the prophets and men of G-d were good Muslims.

Muslims believe that they replace Israel in its calling to be the light to the world. Not only do they believe they replace Israel, but they also believe that the infidels have usurped the original plan of G-d. As the Koran says in 5:44 "It was we who revealed the Torah. By its standard, the prophets judged the Jews, and the prophets bowed (in Islam) to Allah's will, surrendering. For the rabbis and priests: to them was entrusted the protection of

Allah's Scripture Book; they were witnesses of it. Therefore fear not men, but fear Me, and sell not My revelations for a miserable price.".... [5:51] "O you who believe, do not take Jews and Christians as allies; these are allies of one another. Those among you who ally themselves with these belong with them. God does not guide the transgressors. ... [5:82], you will find that the worst enemies of the believers are the Jews and the idol worshipers. And you will find that the closest people in friendship to the believers are those who say, "We are Christians." This is because they have priests and monks among them, and they are not arrogant."

33:26 "Allah made the Jews leave their homes by terrorizing them so that you killed some and made many captive. And He made you inherit their lands, their homes, and their wealth. He gave you a country you had not traversed before."

According to Muslims, the result of our disobedience to the Koran is:

"Mohammed said in his Hadith: 'The Hour [Day of Resurrection] will not arrive until you fight the Jews, [until a Jew will hide behind a rock or tree] and the rock and the tree will say: Oh Muslim, servant of Allah, there is a Jew behind me, come and kill him!'"

This is so, because we read in the Hadith:

Ishaq:240 "The Jews are a nation of liars.... The Jews are a treacherous, lying, and evil people."

Ishaq:250 "The bestial transformation occurred when Allah turned Jews into apes, despised."

Ishaq:245 "Do you love Jews and their religion, you liver-hearted ass, and not Muhammad? Their religion will never march with ours.... Jews make false professions about Islam. So Allah sent down: 'Satan wishes to lead them astray.'"

The Qur'an even mentions that the followers of Jesus (Yeshua) referred to themselves as Muslims.

Then when Isa (Yeshua) came to know of their disbelief, he said: "Who will be my helpers in Allah's cause?" Al-Hawariyyun (disciples of Jesus) said: "We are the helpers of Allah; we believe in Allah, and bear witness that we are Muslims. Our Lord! We believe in what You have sent down, and we follow the Messenger (Yeshua); so write us down among those who bear witness." (Al-Imran, 52 - 53)

There is no doubt that Islam looks at the Jews and Israel as an accursed people, because they refused to accept the revelation of Mohammed.

But the word of Lord is very clear about Israel's place in the mind and heart of G-d.

Jeremiah 31:31-40 "Behold, days are coming," declares the LORD, "when I will make a new covenant with the house of Israel and with the house of Judah, not like the covenant which I made with their fathers in the day I took them by the hand to bring them out of the land of Egypt, My covenant which they broke, although I was a husband to them," declares the LORD. "But this is the covenant which I will make with the house of Israel after those days," declares the LORD, "I will put My law within them and on their heart I will write it; and I will be their G-d, and they shall be My people. They will not teach again, each man his neighbor and each man his brother, saying, 'Know the LORD,' for they will all know Me, from the least of them to the greatest of them," declares the LORD, "for I will forgive their iniquity, and their sin I will remember no more." Thus says the LORD, "Who gives the sun for light by day and the fixed order of the moon and the stars for light by night, Who stirs up the sea so that its waves roar; The LORD of hosts is His name: "If this fixed order departs from before Me," declares the LORD, "then the offspring of Israel also will cease from being a nation before Me forever." Thus says the LORD, "If the heavens above can be measured and the foundations of the earth searched out below, then I will also cast off all the offspring of Israel for all that they have done," declares the LORD. "Behold, days are coming," declares the LORD, "when the city will be rebuilt for the LORD from the Tower of Hananel to the Corner Gate. The measuring line will go out farther straight ahead to the hill Gareb; then it will turn to Goah. And the whole valley of the dead bodies and of the ashes, and all the fields as far as the brook Kidron, to the corner of the Horse Gate toward the east, shall be holy to the LORD; it will not be plucked up or overthrown anymore forever."

In this passage we are told that G-d will make a new covenant with Israel and Judah. The nation will be made whole again. He will then establish Jerusalem, and they will not be "plucked up or overthrown anymore forever." He also says that he will do away with the sun, moon, and stars before He does away with Israel as a nation from before Him.

How do I know this is true? Well, duh—Israel is still here after 4,000 years! There is one more point that has to be brought out in reference to this scripture. After this passage, in which Jeremiah makes this audacious claim, he gives us some information that absolutely confirms the Lord's authority and backs up His ability to keep Israel in its upheld place.

Jeremiah gives us a little glimpse, a snippet, of the Lord's eternal power, which backs up His claim by declaring something only He knows.

Jeremiah 31:35-36 Thus says the LORD, "Who gives the sun for light by day and the fixed order of the moon and the stars for light by night? Who stirs up the sea so that its waves roar; The LORD of hosts is His name: "If this fixed order departs from before Me," declares the LORD, "then the offspring of Israel also will cease from being a nation before Me forever."

You see, this "fixed order of the moon and stars, which stirs up the sea so that it's waves roar" is the articulation of the gravitational pull of the moon on the tides. Please tell me, if you can, who knew this concept back in Jeremiah's time, approximately 600 years B.C? The Lord was and is able to make these claims, based upon who He is and what He knows. He is **El Shaddai**, Lord G-d Almighty. He knows all, He is all powerful, and He is everywhere all at once. He gives us information that only He knows, and then saves it for us in this prophetic display for our benefit 2,600 years later. Because of what the Lord did then, we know He is able to do all that He said for us today. He said He would preserve Israel, and I believe it.

Stan Goodenough stated similar sentiments in an internet article on Friday, 13 June, 2008, on Jerusalem Newswire, list@jnewswire.com.

> "It has everything to do with Israel. For, as I believe we shall see, G-d never gave up on His dream, not even for a second.
>
> After being so sorely betrayed by the creatures He loves, and having His creation spoiled by the one who hates Him with every fiber of his being, G-d put into process a perfect plan to restore men and women in their relationship to Himself, and to restore all things back to the perfect unspoiled way in which He made it at the first.
>
> Israel is the agent through which G-d destined this restoration and redemption to take place. The Land of Israel - G-d"s Holy Land (Zechariah 2:12) - was designated the stage upon which the main act in this drama would be played out. The People of Israel—G-d"s Chosen People (Deuteronomy 7:6)—were consecrated as the cast at the center of the play.
>
> In this land, through this nation, G-d"s plan is unfolding as He determined it should.
>
> And in the end, when Israel has done everything it has been called to do, creation will be remade as it was at the start, and G-d will again see that „it is very good." As will we."

We must be careful to not confuse Israel as G-d's chosen people with an ideology of favoritism. I cannot emphasize enough that they were chosen/created for the benefit of the world. It would behoove Gentile believers to want to see Israel preserved for their own good. For if G-d is not able to keep His promises to Israel, then what makes Gentile believers think that He is able to keep His promises to them?

As I wrote above, Israel is a family that was given a religion and then made a nation. When we really understand the fullness of Romans 9, 10, and 11, we can see how important it is to know as much as possible about the family into which we have been adopted. As a brother in my congregation once said, "Why wouldn't you want to know everything you could about your adopted family's dynamic?" This would include its history, culture, language, and idioms. If the family has functioned successfully, would it benefit you to try and change any of the above? Why would you want to replace the original children of the family that you were adopted into? Wouldn't this show contempt for the family? Wouldn't this also show the fickle nature of the father? If the father gave up on the natural-born children, what would make the adopted children confident that he would not do the same to them?

When we look at the parable of the prodigal son in Luke, we can see that this family's dynamics are a very valid parallel to modern day Israel.

> Luke 15:11-24 And He said, "A man had two sons. The younger of them said to his father, 'Father, give me the share of the estate that falls to me.' So he divided his wealth between them. And not many days later, the younger son gathered everything together and went on a journey into a distant country, and there he squandered his estate with loose living. Now when he had spent everything, a severe famine occurred in that country, and he began to be impoverished. So he went and hired himself out to one of the citizens of that country, and he sent him into his fields to feed swine. And he would have gladly filled his stomach with the pods that the swine were eating, and no one was giving anything to him. But when he came to his senses, he

said, 'How many of my father's hired men have more than enough
bread, but I am dying here with hunger! I will get up and go to my
father, and will say to him, 'Father, I have sinned against heaven, and
in your sight; I am no longer worthy to be called your son; make me
as one of your hired men.' So he got up and came to his father. But
while he was still a long way off, his father saw him and felt compassion for him, and ran and embraced him and kissed him. And the son
said to him, 'Father, I have sinned against heaven and in your sight; I
am no longer worthy to be called your son.' But the father said to his
slaves, 'Quickly bring out the best robe and put it on him, and put a
ring on his hand and sandals on his feet; and bring the fattened calf,
kill it, and let us eat and celebrate; for this son of mine was dead and
has come to life again; he was lost and has been found.'"

Even though the Prodigal left his father's house to squander
his inheritance, he never ceased being a son of the father. Yet,
while he was out in the world, he did not enjoy the continued
protection of the father. When he left, he actually received only a
portion of his potential inheritance. Do we not think that the
father's estate continued to grow in its prosperity? Did the son
not enjoy the privileges of that estate while he stayed at home?
His needs were totally provided for, and he was under the
protection of the father's home. When he left, he lost all of those
privileges. If he had died outside the father's home, he would not
have received a proper burial. His inheritance ceased growing. He
was on his own.

Just like the prodigal son, the nation of Israel too will never
stop being the children of G-d. But just like the prodigal, they
received only a partial inheritance. The part they have missed is
salvation. Until they come home to their Father and realize their
need for His grace, they will always be outside the full protection
of the Father. Yet He waits for His son to come home, and He
will even run out to meet him as soon as He sees him.

Luke 15:20 And he arose and came to his father. But when he was still a great way off, his father saw him and had compassion, and ran and fell on his neck and kissed him.

G-d has a plan for the future of Abraham's children, and He has laid out that plan in a very clear and concise way. This plan has been articulated in the Word, and shows the deep connection between Israel and the entire rest of the world.

2 Sam. 7:22	The Lord has established Israel as His people forever.
Jer. 10:14-16	Israel is the tribe of His inheritance.
Joel 2:18-27	The Lord will be zealous for His land.
Joel 3:1-21	The nations will be judged; Israel will be restored.
Jer. 31:35-36	The descendants of Israel will never cease to be a nation before G-d.
Is. 62:6-7	G-d will establish Jerusalem as the most praised place in all the earth.

All of these promises are for the benefit of the world, not just Israel. For it is through these promises that the Lord established a people for His glory to be spread out to the entire world.

Although Israel displaced the seven ungodly, immoral Canaanite nations to take their G-d-given inheritance of their land, the countries surrounding Israel did not give up the portions of their own land for the establishment of Israel. This land is part of their G-d-appointed inheritance. The Lord gave them this land; and to the rest of the nations, He apportioned land in conjunction with the borders of Israel.

Deuteronomy. 32:8-9 When the Most High gave to the nations their inheritance, when He separated the children of men, He set the bounds of the peoples according to the number of the children of

Israel. For Jehovah's portion is his people; Jacob is the lot of his inheritance.

Joshua 14:1 Now these are the territories which the sons of Israel inherited in the land of Canaan, which Eleazar the priest, and Joshua the son of Nun, and the heads of the households of the tribes of the sons of Israel apportioned to them for an inheritance.

Joshua 23:1-5 Now it came about after many days, when the LORD had given rest to Israel from all their enemies on every side, and Joshua was old, advanced in years, that Joshua called for all Israel, for their elders and their heads and their judges and their officers, and said to them, "I am old, advanced in years, and you have seen all that the LORD your G-d has done to all these nations because of you, for the LORD your G-d is He who has been fighting for you. See, I have apportioned to you these nations which remain as an inheritance for your tribes, with all the nations which I have cut off, from the Jordan even to the Great Sea toward the setting of the sun. The LORD your G-d, He will thrust them out from before you and drive them from before you; and you will possess their land, just as the LORD your G-d promised you."

Psalm 78:55 He also drove out the nations before them and apportioned them for an inheritance by measurement, and made the tribes of Israel dwell in their tents.

This is why Israel is so unique in its creation. They were made by the hand of the Lord Himself. He is their Creator, and He is the one who can and will maintain them according to His Word. Israel is the family into which G-d wants to adopt the Gentiles. If you are a non-Jew, be grateful that he sought you out, and did this all for you. The Lord wants to fulfill His original intent and reconcile the entire world back unto Himself. Israel is His tool and timepiece that He uses to accomplish this, whether anyone else likes it or not. The Jewish context of the Gospel is not just an element that adds color and flavor to the message; it is the message.

Ephesians2:11-22 Therefore remember that formerly you, the Gentiles in the flesh, who are called "Uncircumcision" by the so-called "Circumcision," which is performed in the flesh by human hands— remember that you were at that time separate from Mashiach, excluded from the commonwealth of Israel, and strangers to the covenants of promise, having no hope and without G-d in the world. **But now in Mashiach Yeshua you who formerly were far off have been brought near by the blood of Mashiach.** For He Himself is our peace, who made both groups into one and broke down the barrier of the dividing wall, by abolishing in His flesh the enmity, which is the Law of commandments contained in ordinances, so that in Himself He might make the two into one new man, thus establishing peace, and might reconcile them both in one body to G-d through the cross, by it having put to death the enmity. And He came and preached peace to you who were far away, and peace to those who were near; for through Him we both have our access in one Spirit to the Father. So then you are no longer strangers and aliens, but you are fellow citizens with the saints, and are of   G-d"s household, having been built on the foundation of the apostles and prophets, Mashiach Yeshua Himself being the cornerstone, in whom the whole building, being fitted together, is growing into a holy temple in the Lord, in whom you also are being built together into a dwelling of G-d in the Spirit.

Chapter 6:
So What Have We Learned So Far?

As we have concluded, the Lord chose/created/commissioned Abraham to be a light to the Gentiles—to serve them, so to speak. Abraham, his son, and his grandson were the patriarchs of the Lord's people. From the patriarchs would come the twelve tribes of Israel. Then, from Israel would come Moses, who would give us the law and bring a lawless people back to G-d.

> Galatians 3:17-19 What I am saying is this: the Law, which came four hundred and thirty years later, does not invalidate a covenant previously ratified by G-d, so as to nullify the promise. For if the inheritance is based on law, it is no longer based on a promise; but G-d has granted it to Abraham by means of a promise. **Why the Law then? It was added because of transgressions,** having been ordained through angels by the agency of a mediator, until the seed would come to whom the promise had been made.

This law—the Torah—was given to bring us back to the original covenant and desire of G-d; His original covenant with Abraham—a Covenant of Grace. This grace was not intended for Israel alone, but it was to be extended to the whole world. Abraham was the father of a family that was exalted because of their relationship with G-d, and they eventually became a whole nation. But their status as a family was the most important aspect of who the individuals were. It was because of the family status of Israel that the Gentiles received the Lord's extended hand of grace and fellowship. They were adopted into the family of Israel, but they were not to replace the original children, or the covenant, that was made with Israel. This also meant that they didn't inherit the land that was given to Israel while this earth still stands in its present state because this inheritance was intended for—and promised to—Israel, where they could live apart from the nations, dedicated to the Lord. Gentiles are also not obligated to keep the covenant of law for their salvation. Yet, this does not give them the freedom to live lawless, godless lives.

In first Timothy it says this about the law:

> 1Tim. 1:8-11 But we know that the Law is good, if one uses it lawfully, realizing the fact that law is not made for a righteous person, but for those who are lawless and rebellious, for the ungodly and sinners, for the unholy and profane, for those who kill their fathers or mothers, for murderers and immoral men and homosexuals and kidnappers and liars and perjurers, and whatever else is contrary to sound teaching, according to the glorious gospel of the blessed G-d, with which I have been entrusted.

When an adopted child enters a family, he celebrates with that family just as if they were his own. He doesn't dictate to the family of adoption that they should change their family memorials, rules, and customs just to accommodate him and his past. This act would truly show contempt for the family, which extended a hand of grace to receive him.

The adopted child's entrance into the family was initiated by love and grace. His continuance into a healthy relationship with the family is based on his association with the family dynamic. This family's dynamic is the Torah/instruction. Therefore, he keeps it to remain in healthy relationship with his adopted family.

Unfortunately, this is what many in the "Church" have done. In their attempt to usurp the natural-born children, they have tried to change the entire family dynamic and replace all of the family celebrations and symbols with ones from their own pagan past.

52

The Scripture says that Abraham was called the first "Hebrew." Although there is some difference of opinion, the word "Hebrew" most likely means, "one who has crossed over,‖ from the root word, *avar*. G-d calls him a Hebrew because he crossed over from his former geographical area to reach the land of Canaan. But by defining him as a Hebrew, the Lord also intended for us to learn that a Hebrew is one who has crossed over from his former life (in this case one of idolatry) to living the new life into which the Lord has called him. Knowing this may shed new light on the Biblical reference to Abraham as "our father." He is literally the father of all of his physical descendants, but he is also the father of all who have spiritually crossed over from darkness into the light of the good news of Yeshua." (*Torah Rediscovered*, by Ariel and D'vorah Berkowitz, Shoreshim Publishing, Inc. pages 40 and 41)

That being said, the Gentile believer has to ask himself this question: If he has crossed over, like Abraham, and has been graciously brought into the family by the Lord, why would he try and usurp the natural-born children and then attempt to change the very family he desired to be adopted into with his past pagan practices? Those are the things that they should have left behind.

Change is good?

All my life as a believer, I have been told by too many people: "You're not a Jew anymore; you have converted;" as if to say that the Jewish Messiah, who was promised to me through my own scriptural prophets, also converted and He is no longer a Jew. I will have to say that I don't really remember my conversion event. I have to point out that my Messiah, Yeshua, the hope of Israel, the promised one, the lion of the tribe of Judah, never said to any one, especially to Jews: 'Come, *convert to Christianity*, and follow me.'

What"s in a name?

Yeshua's name never was, and never will be, "Jesus Christ." He never introduced his mother and father as Mary and Joseph Christ. John the Baptist wasn't a Baptist, after all. How has this Jewish Messiah, and all that He stands for, become a Catholic or Protestant all of a sudden? I have to admit; I can see why Jewish people don't want to think of Him as one of their own. He doesn't even look like a Jew anymore. They are repulsed by the lawlessness. This refusal to acknowledge Him by his Hebrew name is another form of replacement theology. Turning Yeshua into Jesus certainly contributes, in a subtle but very effective way, to the elimination of the Jewish image and heritage of the King of the Jews.

Everyone knows how important and powerful words can be. Even wasted and careless words show something about our character. In the spoken and written word we have the power of life and death. We have seen this throughout history, especially during war. Hitler used his words to bewitch an entire nation, dehumanize the Jews and other population groups, and justify torture and genocide. The Scripture truly shows us the importance of a word, and articulates it in many different ways. Prov. 25:11 states,

> "*Like* apples of gold in settings of silver is a word spoken in right circumstances."

In other words, a word spoken well is precious, sweet, and properly framed in the right context. So the question we have to ask ourselves is: What's in a word? Do we fully realize the potential of words in our lives? Words are so powerful that Scripture uses the analogy of a word to describe Yeshua.

"In the beginning was the Word, and the Word was with G-d, and the Word was G-d." (John 1:1)

We express who we are through our words. So Yeshua, the Word of G-d, expresses the very essence of who G-d is.

John 1:14 "And the Word became flesh, and dwelt among us, and we saw His glory, glory as of the only begotten from the Father, full of grace and truth."

Since from Scripture we are able to see and understand the true power of a word, we should never be careless in the use of words. With this point duly noted, we must ask one more question: Are the words we use to speak about G-d important? If so, then a careful examination of our modern use of Biblical names and events must be conducted. If words represent something, then we need to see how they affect us. We need to understand how we think about a topic with their use.

There are different ways to think about things based upon our culture and the words we use to express ideas. This is not limited only to the literal meanings of words, but also to idioms and cultural expressions. How we apply this is important, because the words we use truly affect the very way we think about things. If certain words misrepresent something, then we become led astray in our perception of the truth.

An example of this, as stated above, would be the name "Jesus." What do we think of when we use that name? In thirty years of ministry to Jews and Gentiles, I have seen it evoke different responses from different people. To Catholics, "Jesus" is the Son of Mary, and the figure they see on the crucifix every time they enter church. Protestants see "Jesus" as the originator of "Christianity," to which all men must convert. Muslims call Him Isa, who is no more than a prophet. Mormons look at "Jesus" as the brother of Lucifer. Jehovah's Witnesses believe He and the archangel Michael are one and the same. Jews look at "Jesus" as the person whose religion has caused them a lot of trouble, including exile, persecution, torture, and murder, for the last 2,000 years.

But if we change the scenario by simply calling Him by His Hebrew name, Yeshua, it changes the entire way we think about Him. He is now a Jewish man with a Jewish identity. He is no longer the perceived originator of a new religion. By calling Him by His Jewish name we have given back to Him the original intent of His culture, religion, geography, etc. He is now a Jew from Israel, not a Catholic from Rome. It is subtle, but I promise, if you call Him by His Jewish name, after a while you will start to think of Him differently. This is more than just an argument over words. Because words have depth, as I said above, their meanings go way beyond just their literal use. Words carry the baggage of the history and cultural nuance in which they are used. Yeshua was never called "Jesus" by anyone of His generation. He was known to His peers by the name Yeshua ha Nazoret (Yeshua the Nazarine), Yeshua ben Yoseph (son of Joseph), or Yeshua ha Mashiach (Yeshua the Messiah).

The name Yeshua means something in Hebrew; it is not just a name. The Lord called him that because it means "salvation." What does the word "Jesus" mean? When was it first used? Was it given as a substitute of His Jewish name for a purpose? Scripture does say that there is only one name under heaven and earth whereby men must be saved. That name would not have been "Jesus."

> Acts 4:12 And there is salvation in no one else; for there is **no other name** under heaven that has been given among men by which we must be saved.

Was there a purpose to this declaration, or was it thrown out carelessly? It does seem to me that the Lord has never wasted words at any time in history. Every word that He spoke had a purpose. G-d gave us the Scriptures and chose His words very carefully for our benefit, so that we might know His Word is true.

> 2Timothy 3:15-17 ... and that from childhood you have known the sacred writings which are able to give you the wisdom that leads to salvation through faith which is in Mashiach Yeshua. All Scripture is inspired by G-d and profitable for teaching, for reproof, for correction, for training in righteousness; so that the man of G-d may be adequate, equipped for every good work.

This is not an argument meant to challenge anyone's salvation. However, once you know the truth and the importance of these words uttered by G-d, how can you ignore this truth? We are saved by grace, but we still have to grow in our faith. If we change the names of all the Biblical characters, especially Yeshua, we change the Gospel from a Jewish message to a "Christian" one. If the Jews, who were commissioned to carry the message of salvation to the Gentiles, no longer recognize it anymore, how can they bear the message? If the Jews no longer recognize Yeshua and His message as Jewish, shouldn't that cause us to be suspicious of how it is communicated and represented by the "Church?"

As a note of interest, "Jesus" did not become "Jesus" until around 1769. You see, there was no *J* consonant pronounced in the English language then. The original 1611 King James Bible wrote his name as Iesus. In the 1769 King James Version it was changed to "Jesus." The first English-language book to make a clear distinction between *i* and *j* was published in 1634.

Was Yeshua a Greek or a Jew? Did He speak Hebrew, Latin, Greek, or King James Elizabethan English? All these very subtle, linguistic nuances make a huge difference in how we perceive His message and identity. We need to be very careful with G-d's message to us in Scripture, weighing every word of His, and heeding His warnings that He gives us.

> Deuteronomy 18:18-20 It shall come about that whoever will not listen to My words which he shall speak in My name, I Myself will require it of him. But the prophet who speaks a word presumptuous-ly in My name which I have not commanded him to speak, or which he speaks in the name of other gods, that prophet shall die.

> Deuteronomy 4:2 You shall not add to the word which I am com-manding you, nor take away from it, that you may keep the com-mandments of the LORD your G-d which I command you.

> Deuteronomy 12:32 Whatever I command you, you shall be careful to do; you shall not add to nor take away from it.

> Proverbs 30:5-6 Every Word of G-d is tested; He is a shield to those who take refuge in Him. Do not add to His words, or He will re-prove you, and you will be proved a liar.

Chapter 7:
Who Did It?

For over 1,700 years, the "Church" has been on a mission to convert/proselytize the Jewish people into the "Christian" faith. The "Church" presents the idea to the Jews that when they come to their own Messiah, they perform a non-Jewish, foreign conversion. It amazes me that every group seeking the conversion of the Jews tries to absorb them into their particular sect, and more or less Gentilize, as well as Christianize, them. That which was meant to be natural for the Jew has become the "essential other." The family has been changed and doesn't look the same as it was meant. Trying not to be too critical, I have to ask the question of the church: Is this how "Christianity" was meant to look like from its first century form?

When Yeshua comes back, will he look at the "Church" and say to them, "What have you done to my congregation? Nothing looks the same as when I was here!"

As a brother in my congregation said, "Cain was a man who had a direct revelation of G-d in his life. He heard the voice of G-d, and his response was still negative. G-d gave him more than ample opportunity to do what was right, and he refused. This was as a result of his pride and anger. The Lord showed His willingness to redeem, and Cain showed his refusal to be redeemed".

> Genesis 4:3-7 So it came about in the course of time that Cain brought an offering to the LORD of the fruit of the ground. Abel, on his part also brought of the firstlings of his flock and of their fat portions. And the LORD had regard for Abel and for his offering; but

for Cain and for his offering He had no regard. So Cain became very
angry and his countenance fell. Then the LORD said to Cain, "Why
are you angry? And why has your countenance fallen? If you do well,
will not your countenance be lifted up? And if you do not do well, sin
is crouching at the door; and its desire is for you, but you must mas-
ter it."

Cain was fully determined to tell G-d a lie. He was so deceived by his sin that he really thought he could pull a fast one
over on G-d. For too long "Christians" have offered the sacrifice
of Cain to G-d. They bring Him whatever they want to, not what
He asks. Is this in spite of the fact that they know the truth? Or
are they so deceived that they are unable to see the truth?

"Christianity" has taken all that Yeshua did and celebrated as
prophetic displays, and synchronized these memorials into pagan
rituals in an attempt to change the family dynamic, and replaced
these wonderful, G-d-given celebrations with the pagan rituals of
foreign deities.

Christians have replaced Sukkot (Tabernacles), the festival
which represents G-d dwelling among man for 40 years in the
wilderness, with Christmas. They have separated the time of
Yeshua's resurrection from Passover, and called it Easter. The
Passover, so spiritually rich and full of prophetic display, has now
been relegated to the pile of "Jewish events which we are set free
from," because, as I repeatedly hear from good "Church" folks,
"we are no longer under the (curse of the) law." Therefore, they
feel free to live lives of lawlessness and make it up as they go
along.

When Christians claim the blood of Yeshua, do they really
understand why blood atonement is necessary? They cannot,
unless they understand the Jewish holy day of Yom Kippur,
mentioned in Leviticus 17. All of the allusions to the blood

sacrifice show to us its ultimate fulfillment in Yeshua. It is necessary to know about the Jewish Yom Teru'ah, or Rosh Hashanah, in order to understand the end times.

How do we know about these Biblical events? It is not just through reading about them in a book, or being able to quote a verse and chapter from the Bible. We need to experience them in order for them to become part of our lives. We need first-hand, experiential knowledge of these events to make them real in our lives. This is why we celebrate; not to keep the law for our salvation, but to remember, memorialize, and celebrate what G-d has done for us in the past, present, and future.

These holy days are our heritage and promises from the Lord. Yeshua fulfills them all. Do we think that the Lord just gave us a list of things to make, do, and keep busy with, so we would stay out of trouble? Scripture calls them "moadim"—appointed times and seasons. These were appointed by the Lord as Holy Convocations. They were very specific because each and every one of the festivals prophesied Yeshua.

> Leviticus 23:1-2 The LORD spoke again to Moses, saying, "Speak to the sons of Israel and say to them, 'The LORD's appointed times which you shall proclaim as holy convocations—My appointed times are these:'"

Does it not seem right to keep an appointment with G-d? On the other hand, doesn't it seem suspicious to change even one of those appointments, substituting it with something else?

These holy days were appointments that could be kept only by Yeshua Himself. They are very specific, prophetic, and given by the Lord as signs of His relationship with mankind, and His future day of judgment. The reason why we celebrate them is that they are memorials of the very incarnation and resurrection of the

Messiah Himself. If you don't celebrate them, you have to invent a memorial that has neither prophetic root nor foundation, like Christmas or Easter. Why should I have anything to do with a pagan holiday? I prefer to celebrate the death, burial, and resurrection on Passover and First Fruits, the holy days that prophetically speak of these events. I celebrate the incarnation of Yeshua during Succot, the holy day that celebrates the Lord dwelling among men for forty years while they were wandering in the wilderness, after their exodus from Egypt.

So, the original intent of the moadim was to have them be appointed prophetic symbols and fulfillments given by the Lord to His people for their own commemoration of His salvation, but also given in order to draw believing Gentiles to Himself for their own redemption. However, "Christians" took these moadim and decided that these appointments needed to be altered in order to accommodate their original pagan lives and cultures. They then decided that these pagan celebrations are better than the original moadim, and replaced them totally, all under the banner of, "We have been set free from the curse of the law." These people had no clue what it meant to live "under the law;" so, therefore, they felt at liberty to live lives of complete lawlessness.

When Yeshua rebuked the Scribes and Pharisees in Matthew 23, it was not because they were keepers of the law; it was because of their hypocrisy.

> Matthew 23:1-3 Then Jesus (Yeshua) spoke to the crowds and to His disciples, saying: "The scribes and the Pharisees have seated themselves in the chair of Moses; therefore, all that they tell you, do and observe, but do not do according to their deeds; for they say things and do not do them. "

Another translation of this verse, written in Shem Tov's Hebrew translation of Matthew, states it like this: (A complete Hebrew text of Matthew that appeared in the body of the 14th century Jewish polemic treatise entitled *Even Bohan "The Touchstone."* The author is Shem-Tob ben-Isaac ben-Shaprut).

"The Pharisees and sages sit upon the seat of Moses. Therefore, all that he says to you, diligently do, but according to their reforms and their precedents do not do, because they talk, but they do not do."

In the Hebrew Matthew, Yeshua is telling His disciples not to obey the Pharisees. If their claim to authority is that they sit in Moses' seat, then they should diligently do as Moses tells us to do! They took upon themselves an authority that was not theirs. They wrested the authority of the Priesthood and made judgments that were reserved for the Messiah when He was to come.

Another point:

In Matthew 5:17-20, we read:

Do not think that I came to abolish the Law or the Prophets; I did not come to abolish but to fulfill. For truly I say to you, until heaven and earth pass away, not the smallest letter or stroke shall pass from the Law until all is accomplished. Whoever then annuls one of the least of these commandments, and teaches others to do the same, shall be called least in the kingdom of heaven; but whoever keeps and teaches them, he shall be called great in the kingdom of heaven. For I say to you that unless your righteousness surpasses that of the scribes and Pharisees, you will not enter the kingdom of heaven.

Here Yeshua makes a statement seemingly divergent from traditional modern church doctrine. If the Messiah did not come to abolish but to fulfill, how can the church maintain that we are set free from the law? The confusion lies in our understanding of what it means to fulfill. Fulfill does not mean to abrogate and do away with, but to show its true meaning and intent. That which was once concealed is now clarified and explained fully. It was always the understanding of the Rabbis that when the Messiah came it would be His right to interpret the Torah in its fullness. This is based upon their interpretation of Jeremiah 31:31-33

> "Behold, days are coming," declares the LORD, "when I will make a new covenant with the house of Israel and with the house of Judah, not like the covenant which I made with their fathers in the day I took them by the hand to bring them out of the land of Egypt, My covenant, which they broke, although I was a husband to them," declares the LORD. "But this is the covenant which I will make with the house of Israel after those days," declares the LORD, "I will put My law within them and on their heart I will write it; and I will be their G-d, and they shall be My people."

When Yeshua came, he did exactly that. He put the law in our hearts. As I have said before, I say again—the law has not been abolished; it has been fulfilled. The law is now where it should have been from the beginning—in our hearts.

In Matthew chapter 5, Yeshua does exactly what the Rabbis said the Messiah would do. He interprets the law in accordance with the true intent of the law and invests in Himself the sole authority to do so. After he tells us, **"I did not come to abolish but to fulfill,"** He then starts the process of fulfilling it in verse 21 and 22 by making a statement that no ordinary Rabbi had the right to make.

> "You have heard that the ancients were told... But I say to you..."

The point that I am making here is that any Rabbi (lit. teacher) of Yeshua's time, and beyond that, was supposed to hand down interpretations in the name of his Rabbis and their preceding Rabbis, who according to tradition, derived their interpretations from Moses' explanations of Scripture from G-d on Mt. Sinai. No one was allowed to interpret Scripture in his own name.

Yet Yeshua does exactly this, showing that He had authority above the Scribes and Pharisaic Rabbis. Who was He that He would dare interpret Scripture on His own? He was the Messiah, of course. This is why, when He finishes the Sermon on the Mount, we read:

> Matthew 7:28-29 When Yeshua had finished these words, the crowds were amazed at His teaching; for He was teaching them as one having authority, and not as their scribes.

It was not for the abrogation of the law that Yeshua came, it was for the fulfillment. Now our task is to understand what that means for believers, both Jew and Gentile.

Chapter 8:
Don't You Forget to Tithe

Mentioned 18 times in the Scripture

I find it rather odd that so many in the "Church" who invalidate the concept of the keeping the Torah, under the guise of the false argument of grace verses law, still demand that the tithe is valid. It would seem to me that if the law was abolished, as they say, then would it not also make sense that the principle of the tithe would follow suit? After all, the tithe does originate in the "Old Testament" Law. As a matter of fact, it predates the law. The first mention of the tithe is found in Genesis 14:17-20. This was when Avraham went to rescue his nephew Lot from Chedorlaomer, king of Elam.

> Then after his return from the defeat of Chedorlaomer and the kings who were with him, the king of Sodom went out to meet him at the valley of Shaveh (that is, the King's Valley). And Melchizedek, king of Salem, brought out bread and wine; now he was a priest of God Most High. He blessed him and said,
> "Blessed be Abram of God Most High,
> Possessor of heaven and earth;
> And blessed be God Most High,
> Who has delivered your enemies into your hand."
> He gave him a tenth of all.

It would seem that this Melchizedek, King of Salem (Peace), not only knew about the one true Lord, but was also a priest. So there were other people at the time of Avram who knew of the Lord. Why would Avram give him a tenth of all? What was his motivation for that response?

Melchizedek is mentioned ten times in the Scripture.

Psalm 110

A Psalm of David

1   The LORD says to my Lord:
    "Sit at My right hand
    Until I make Your enemies a footstool for Your feet."
2   The LORD will stretch forth Your strong scepter from Zion,
    saying, "Rule in the midst of Your enemies."
3   Your people will volunteer freely in the day of Your power;
    In holy array, from the womb of the dawn,
    Your youth are to You *as* the dew.
4   The LORD has sworn and will not change His mind,
    You are a priest forever according to the order of Melchizedek.
5   The Lord is at Your right hand;
    He will shatter kings in the day of His wrath.
6   He will judge among the nations,
    He will fill *them* with corpses,
    He will shatter the chief men over a broad country.
7   He will drink from the brook by the wayside;
    Therefore He will lift up *His* head.

This Melchizedek (or in Hebrew, Melechtzadic), King of Salem, King of Righteousness, must have been a pretty important character for Avram to tithe to and for King David to mention like he did. And who is this Lord in the Psalms that will have his enemies put under his feet, whose scepter from Zion will rule in the midst of his enemies? Who is this Lord who is a priest after the order of Melchizedek? The goal of this chapter is not intended to unravel the mystery of Melchizedek and his identity. The point I want to make is that he is a very important figure as a priest of the Lord, and that he is worthy of receiving the tithe from Avram. The Lord sets a precedent here; the tithe goes to a priest. Again, let me emphasize that this concept of tithing predated the giving of the law. The tithe was given specifically to an **appointed** priest of the Lord. We see that it is articulated in much greater detail in the Law.

The next time the tithe is mentioned is in Leviticus 27:30-32:

> Thus all the tithe of the land, of the seed of the land, or of the fruit of the tree, is the LORD'S; it is holy to the LORD. If, therefore, a man wishes to redeem part of his tithe, he shall add to it one-fifth of it. For every tenth part of herd or flock, whatever passes under the rod, the tenth one shall be holy to the LORD.

What we also notice is that the tithe is agricultural and pastoral. They were to give from what they produced. The tithe was not a monetary principle or demand.

And then in Numbers 18:21-24:

> To the sons of Levi, behold, I have given all the tithe in Israel for an inheritance, in return for their service which they perform, the service of the tent of meeting. The sons of Israel shall not come near the tent of meeting again, or they will bear sin and die. Only the Levites shall perform the service of the tent of meeting, and they shall bear their iniquity; it shall be a perpetual statute throughout your generations, and among the sons of Israel they shall have no inheritance. For the tithe of the sons of Israel, which they offer as an offering to the LORD, I have given to the Levites for an inheritance; therefore I have said concerning them, "They shall have no inheritance among the sons of Israel."

The tithe was given to the Levites because they had no inheritance. This was a perpetual statute. They served in the Temple. They were a priestly tribe appointed by the Lord. They were not self-appointed pastors that assumed they had the right to usurp the Lord's appointed priesthood and collect finances in the name of their supposed inherited authority.

> Then the LORD spoke to Moses, saying, "Moreover, you shall speak to the Levites and say to them, 'When you take from the sons of Israel the tithe which I have given you from them for your inheritance, then you shall present an offering from it to the LORD, a tithe of the tithe. Your offering shall be reckoned to you as the grain from the

threshing floor or the full produce from the wine vat. So you shall also present an offering to the LORD from your tithes, which you receive from the sons of Israel; and from it you shall give the LORD'S offering to Aaron the priest."

The Levites were also to tithe from what they received and give it to Aaron and his descendants. They were also to present it as an offering to the Lord. I sure don't see that happening today in the churches.

> Deuteronomy 12:17-19 You are not allowed to eat within your gates the tithe of your grain or new wine or oil, or the firstborn of your herd or flock, or any of your votive offerings which you vow, or your freewill offerings, or the contribution of your hand. But you shall eat them before the LORD your God in the place which the LORD your God will choose, you and your son and daughter, and your male and female servants, and the Levite who is within your gates; and you shall rejoice before the LORD your God in all your undertakings. Be careful that you do not forsake the Levite as long as you live in your land.

The instructions for the tithe were very specific, not generic. There was a time and place for the tithe. The tithe was also to be enjoyed by the giver. Where do we see this happening today? When is the last time you were invited to rejoice before the Lord and also partake in the tithe?

> Deuteronomy 14:23-29 You shall surely tithe all the produce from what you sow, which comes out of the field every year. You shall eat in the presence of the LORD your God, at the place where He chooses to establish His name, the tithe of your grain, your new wine, your oil, and the firstborn of your herd and your flock, so that you may learn to fear the LORD your God always. If the distance is so great for you that you are not able to bring the tithe, since the place where the LORD your God chooses to set His name is too far away from you when the LORD your God blesses you, then you shall exchange it for money, and bind the money in your hand and go to the place which the LORD your God chooses. You may spend the money for whatever your heart desires: for oxen, or sheep, or wine, or strong drink, or whatever your heart desires; and there you shall eat in the presence of the LORD your God and rejoice, you and your

household. Also you shall not neglect the Levite who is in your town, for he has no portion or inheritance among you.

At the end of every third year you shall bring out all the tithe of your produce in that year, and shall deposit it in your town. The Levite, because he has no portion or inheritance among you, and the alien, the orphan and the widow who are in your town, shall come and eat and be satisfied, in order that the LORD your God may bless you in all the work of your hand which you do.

We eat it in Jerusalem and you could exchange it for money, if coming to Jerusalem with your flock was too far. The third year it was to be given to the local community, to the widows, orphans, aliens, fatherless, and strangers, the "ger toshav" (the sojourner) who sojourned among you.

> Deuteronomy 26:12-15 When you have finished paying all the tithe **of your increase** in the third year, the year of tithing, then you shall give it to the Levite, to the stranger, to the orphan and to the widow that they may eat in your towns and be satisfied. You shall say before the LORD your God, "I have removed the sacred *portion* from *my* house, and also have given it to the Levite and the alien, the orphan and the widow, according to all Your commandments which You have commanded me; I have not transgressed or forgotten any of Your commandments. I have not eaten of it while mourning, nor have I removed any of it while I was unclean, nor offered any of it to the dead. I have listened to the voice of the LORD my God; I have done according to all that You have commanded me. Look down from Your holy habitation, from heaven, and bless Your people Israel, and the ground which You have given us, a land flowing with milk and honey, as You swore to our fathers."

We finish paying all of our obligations first. We take care of our families. Then, from the profit, we take a tenth. This is not what is done today at all. The argument I hear mostly is whether we should tithe from our gross or net earnings.

For convenience sake today, the "Church" uses certain selected Scriptures to base their authority to collect the tithe while the rest of the Biblical formula is ignored. They reject what the rest of the Scripture says about tithing. This is one of the Scriptures they will use while ignoring the rest.

> Malachi 3:8-12 "Will a man rob God? Yet you are robbing Me!" But you say, "How have we robbed You?" "In tithes and offerings. You are cursed with a curse, for you are robbing Me, the whole nation *of you!* Bring the whole tithe into the storehouse, so that there may be food in My house, and test Me now in this," says the LORD of hosts, "if I will not open for you the windows of heaven and pour out for you a blessing until it overflows. Then I will rebuke the devourer for you, so that it will not destroy the fruits of the ground; nor will your vine in the field cast *its grapes,*" says the LORD of hosts. "All the nations will call you blessed, for you shall be a delightful land," says the LORD of hosts.

The Lord really meant it when He said bring the tithe into **His storehouse. This was the Temple. Nowhere is it translated "Church."** This is the immediate and correct context of this verse.

Please don't misunderstand me. I am not telling anyone to not tithe. Feel free to take your liberty to tithe. Just go out and find a widow, orphan, Levite, priest, and a Temple in Jerusalem to give your tithe to.

The tithe was as much a public welfare program as it was a way to provide for the needs of the Priests and Levites. The Lord ordained it for a specific purpose, and the use of it today is not synonymous with the intended use in the Scriptures.

If we claim the authority of the Word to back up our doctrines and practices, then should not our claim be consistent with the original intent of the Lord in its use?

This is the real issue I want to bring to our attention. **The church demands that you fulfill the law of the tithe by bringing it to the church. Yet, they refuse to see the rest of the commands involved with the tithe as valid.** It is perfectly acceptable to them to demand the tithe from the people when it fits their need, but when the rest of the laws concerning the tithe contradict church doctrine and practice, it is not convenient.

The "Church" can't have it both ways. They either accept the Word of the Lord in its entirety or not at all.

Using the Lord to endorse a capitalistic agenda is convenient, but not Biblical. Why is it that so many in the "Church" feel they have the right to pick and choose what parts of the Word are valid and what parts are invalid based only on what is convenient for their agenda?

For the "Church" to presume the authority to collect the tithe, they must now see themselves in the position of replacing the Levitical priesthood. This is a very subtle form of replacement theology. If the "Church" feels the right to change the word in this incident, then where will it stop? We are reminded in **Deuteronomy 5** of the Lord's commands to Moses. They were precious and very specific. The things the Lord said, He meant. There was no room for personal interpretation. Neither was there an option to pick and choose one from column A and two from column B. This was not a Chinese menu.

> Deuteronomy 5:30-33 Go, say to them, "Return to your tents." But as for you, stand here by Me, that I may **speak to you all the commandments and the statutes and the judgments which you shall teach them, that they may observe them** in the land which I give them to possess. **So you shall observe to do just as the LORD your God has commanded you; you shall not turn aside to the right or to the left.** You shall walk in all the way which the LORD your God has commanded you, that you may live and that it may be well with you, and that you may prolong *your* days in the land which you will possess.

And for emphasis sake the Lord said it again in chapter 6:1-3.

Obey God and Prosper
Now this is the commandment, the statutes, and the judgments
which the LORD your God has commanded me to teach you,
that you might do them in the land where you are going over to
possess it, so that you and your son and your grandson might fear the
LORD your God, **to keep all His statutes and His command-**
ments which I command you, all the days of your life, and that
your days may be prolonged. O Israel, you should listen and be careful to do *it,* that it may be well with you and that you may multiply
greatly, just as the LORD, the God of your fathers, has promised
you, *in* a land flowing with milk and honey.

So where in the Word of the Lord is it stated that 21st century
western pastors are now the recipients of the tithe? Is it not
obvious that this is, at best, an assumed position built on specula-
tion and silence?

Let me state that I am not auguring the point that people
should not give to the local body offerings from their personal
finances. But these offerings are not the tithe. They are exactly
that—free-will offerings. The point that needs emphasis is that
the "Church" does not have the right to change the Word of the
Lord in any way. They do not have the authority to assume that
the tithe was ever meant for the local church or the pastor's
personal ministry.

If this were the case then wouldn't there be more specific instructions concerning the tithe in the New Covenant Scriptures?
The "Church" is not Israel. Yet, they assume the blessing that the
Lord promised to Israel, but refuse the responsibilities and
requirements to receive those blessings.

Without sounding redundant, this is because the "Church"
has abandoned the Biblical Jewish roots of the faith in order to
make a new faith with whatever they decided to pick and choose

from. The have "boasted against the natural branches" (Rom. 11:17-24).

How then shall we give?

Let's now look at the New Covenant understanding of how to give.

The topic of the tithe is not found in the New Covenant Scriptures. There is no instruction on the giving of the tithe. "Why is that?" you might ask. Because they already knew what it was about; they had the Law and the prophets for instruction (Acts 15).

Yeshua does speak about the tithe but does not give instructions that were already known. He deals with the motivation of the Scribes and Pharisees in their giving.

> Matthew 23:23 Woe to you, scribes and Pharisees, hypocrites! For you tithe mint and dill and cumin, and have neglected the weightier provisions of the law: justice and mercy and faithfulness; but these are the things you should have done without neglecting the others.

> Luke 11:42 But woe to you Pharisees! For you pay tithe of mint and rue and every kind of garden herb, and yet disregard justice and the love of God; but these are the things you should have done without neglecting the others.

In the parable in Luke 18, Yeshua again addresses the motivation of the heart. The point that He is trying to make is that we should be careful not to boast about our righteousness. Religious practices don't make one righteous. The Lord makes us righteous, and when we realize our pitiful state, that's when the Lord can have His way in us.

> Luke 18:11-12 The Pharisee stood and was praying this to himself: "God, I thank You that I am not like other people: swindlers, unjust, adulterers, or even like this tax collector. I fast twice a week; I pay tithes of all that I get.'"

The tithe is also mentioned in Hebrews, but that is to remind us of the incident with Melechtzadic.

> Hebrews 7:7-10 But without any dispute the lesser is blessed by the greater. In this case mortal men receive tithes, but in that case one *receives them*, of whom it is witnessed that he lives on.
> And, so to speak, through Abraham even Levi, who received tithes, paid tithes, for he was still in the loins of his father when Melchizedek met him.

What *is* mentioned in the New Covenant Scriptures is the concept of giving offerings. This is not the tithe. This is also not just a matter of semantics. There is a distinction. I have pointed out above why the tithe was collected and how it was used.

> Acts 24:17 "Now after several years I came to bring alms to my nation and to present offerings;"

Rav Shaul, knowing the law of the tithe, does not apply this law to the giving of offerings in the body of New Covenant believers.

> Matthew 5:24 Therefore, if you are presenting your offering at the altar, and there remember that your brother has something against you, leave your offering there before the altar and go; first be reconciled to your brother, and then come and present your offering.

In reference to this offering of which the Lord speaks, this is still being done in the Temple system. The body of New Covenant believers had not yet been established at that time. Tithes and offerings were still brought to the Temple.

> Acts 4:32 And the congregation of those who believed was of one heart and soul; and not one of them claimed that anything belonging to him was his own, but all things were common property to them.

After the founding of the New Covenant body, they used their resources to spread the Word and sustain this new congregation. What you don't hear in the New Covenant Scriptures in the early life of the believers is the topic of tithing. Nowhere is it found that the Apostles ever went around collecting the tithe that was meant for the Priests, Levites, widows, orphans, and strangers.

> Galatians 2:10 "They only asked us to remember the poor—the very thing I also was eager to do."
>
> Romans 15:25-27 ...but now, I am going to Jerusalem serving the saints. For Macedonia and Achaia have been pleased to make a contribution for the poor among the saints in Jerusalem. Yes, they were pleased to do so, and they are indebted to them. For if the Gentiles have shared in their spiritual things, they are indebted to minister to them also in material things.

Their giving was of a free-will nature. This was not the case for the tithe which was commanded—it was part of the "Law." As was pointed out earlier, the tithe was attached to the Temple ritual. It was agricultural and pastoral. It had a specific purpose and use. "Now that the Messiah has come," as we have been informed by the "Church," "the Torah, and the need to adhere to it, has been abolished." So why should they hold onto this part of the Law and reject the rest? My answer is not a pretty one?

The reason why the "Church" demands the tithe yet rejects the rest of the Law is because it benefits the leadership. It gives pastors job security. It helps to promote the big business nature of the "Church" and keep it in-tact so that it looks like we are really affecting the Kingdom of G-d, when all we are doing is growing our own personal kingdoms and erecting massive edifices for our own legacy.

Since Messiah came His Torah is now written on our hearts, so why should the giving of our offerings be of a different nature. If giving is of a free will nature, it is much harder to project an income flow and have job security. Demanding the tithe also contributes to the idea of replacement theology—the idea that the "Church" now replaces Israel. Only appointed people of the Lord are instructed to collect the tithe. Churches zealously guard that right and authority. That is one benefit you don't want to lose.

This is how Yeshua answered the rich young ruler:

Luke 18:18-23 A ruler questioned Him, saying, "Good Teacher, what shall I do to inherit eternal life?" And Jesus said to him, "Why do you call Me good? No one is good except God alone. You know the commandments, 'Do not commit adultery, do not murder, do not steal, do not bear false witness, honor your father and mother.'"

And he said, "All these things I have kept from *my* youth."

When Jesus heard *this*, He said to him, "One thing you still lack; sell all that you possess and distribute it to the poor, and you shall have treasure in heaven; and come, follow Me."

But when he had heard these things, he became very sad, for he was extremely rich.

Yeshua instructed the rich young ruler to be careful not to put his devotion to riches above his devotion to the Lord. I could end this chapter with the same encouragement. Let me conclude by asking one question: Would the "Church" continue to grow, and the Kingdom of the Lord expand, even if we didn't demand the tithe, but only gave as we could in free will? It might not in America, but it sure does in places where the believers are underground, like China or the Middle East.

So by all means give—give generously and joyfully—but **not** because you obey a system that has usurped Biblical authority. Selah.

Chapter 9:
How Then Shall We Live? As Messianic Jews and Messianic Gentiles.

Do we, as some say, have the freedom to live any way we please? Does being set free from the law mean that we get to make up the rules of living out our faith? Let me again clarify that Scripture clearly emphasizes that salvation is by grace.

> Ephesians 2:8-9 For by grace you have been saved through faith; and that not of yourselves, it is the gift of G-d; not as a result of works, so that no one may boast.

So how we live has nothing to do with gaining salvation. It is a matter of how we grow into the adoptive family that has so graciously accepted us, and whether or not we live in harmony with an already established and well-functioning family. I, for one, am not convinced that the "Church" as we know it today is a healthy representation of what the Lord really expects from his people.

> "There are approximately 38,000 Christian denominations in the world. This statistic takes into consideration cultural distinctions of denominations in different countries." World Christian Encyclopedia (2001).

We have to ask ourselves: Is this what New Covenant believers are supposed to look like? We are fractured and disjointed. If I am a Messianic Jew, which religious tradition should I adopt as the true representation of New Testament faith? Every denomination represents another little piece of the "Church's" dysfunction. We have been so busy trying to make the Gospel relevant to our society, that it has become only a shadow of its former self. This statement is based upon my common observation and the "Church's" not too distant history.

How have we been able to divorce ourselves from the fact that it has only been as recent as the 1940s, in WW2, when Pope Pius XII was an ally of Hitler and did not protest publically against the wholesale, premeditated, deliberate persecution and slaughter of six million Jews?

Can we say that this representation of the "Church" was legitimate? Did their actions stand up to the scriptural mandate of being a light and testimony to this dark world? Some might say, "That was then; it's different now." I might agree with them if it wasn't the modus operandi of their entire history. The Catholic Church has persecuted the Jews in the name of "Jesus" now for over 1,700 years. This happened as a result of abandoning the Biblical Jewish roots of the faith and replacing them with a fabricated doctrine and history. How has the Gospel benefited from the total reckless disregard for the Jewish nature of the Yeshua's message? Here are just few examples of some of the events that transpired over two nearly two millennia of Jewish persecution by Catholics. This information was taken from the web site *www.religioustolerance.org*.

325 A.D.: The *Council of Nicea* separated the celebration of Easter from the Jewish Passover. They stated: "*For it is unbecoming beyond measure that on this holiest of festivals we should follow the customs of the Jews. Henceforth let us have nothing in common with this odious people...We ought not, therefore, to have anything in common with the Jews...our worship follows a...more convenient course...we desire dearest*

*brethren, to separate ourselves from the detestable company of the Jews...How,
then, could we follow these Jews, who are almost certainly blinded."*

337 A.D.: Christian Emperor Constantius created a law which made the marriage of a Jewish man to a Christian punishable by death.

379-395 A.D.: Emperor Theodosius the Great permitted the destruction of synagogues if they served a religious purpose. Christianity became the state religion of the Roman Empire at this time.

528A.D.: Emperor Justinian (527-564) passed the Justinian Code. It prohibited Jews from building synagogues, reading the Bible in Hebrew, assembling in public, celebrating Passover before Easter, and testifying against "Christians" in court.

613 A.D.: Very serious persecution began in Spain. Jews were given the option of either leaving Spain or converting to Christianity. Jewish children over six years of age were taken from their parents and given a Christian education.

1096 A.D.: The first Crusade was launched in this year. Although the prime goal of the crusades was to liberate Jerusalem from the Muslims, Jews were a secondary target. As the soldiers passed through Europe on the way to the Holy Land, large numbers of Jews were challenged: *"Christ-killers, embrace the Cross or die!"* 12,000 Jews in the Rhine Valley alone were killed in the first Crusade. This behavior continued for eight additional crusades until the ninth crusade in 1272.

1099 A.D.: The Crusaders forced all of the Jews of Jerusalem into a central synagogue and set it on fire. Those who tried to escape were forced back into the burning building.

1189 A.D.: Jews were persecuted in England. The Crown claimed all Jewish possessions. Most of their houses were burned.

1229 A.D.: The Spanish Inquisition starts. Later, in 1252, Pope Innocent IV authorizes the use of torture by the Inquisitors.

1290 A.D.: Jews are exiled from England. About 16,000 left the country.

1306 A.D.: 100,000 Jews are exiled from France. They left with only the clothes on their backs and food for only one day.

1320 A.D.: 40,000 French shepherds went to Palestine on the Shepherd Crusade. On the way, 140 Jewish communities were destroyed.

1492 A.D.: Jews were given the choice of being baptized as Christians or be banished from Spain. 300,000 left Spain penniless. Many migrated to Turkey where they found tolerance among the Muslims. Others converted to "Christianity" but often continued to practice Judaism in secret.

This does not do justice, nor does it cover all of the Church's bad treatment of the Jews throughout history. But it does give you a brief taste of what has been done to Jews in the name of their Jewish Messiah.

The world of theology is a murky one. With so many "Chris-Tian" denominations to choose from, it is very hard to discern whose theology is right. We have to ask how these different groups developed their distinctions. I have studied many of the theological camps, and this also includes the major cults. I have discovered one very similar distinctive that most of them share. I have concluded from my observations of Calvinists, Arminianists, Pentecostals, Orthodox, Catholics, and every other group in between, that most of them build their denominational distinctive around just a few specific doctrines. The emphasis tends to be on very specific subjects. Hence they develop their theology by excluding other scriptures which would contradict their theories.

I am not saying that they have developed no other doctrines, but the emphasis is put on just a few, very predominant topics. Here are a few examples: The Calvinists are focused on eternal security and irresistible grace, while the Arminianists focus on the issue of free will and man's obligation to abide in G-d's saving grace; the Pentecostals concentrate on the gifts of the spirit and supernatural manifestations, some concentrating on foreign languages, or "tongues" as their primary gift; others focus on prophesying, while others focus on miraculous healing. Then you have the sub-groups, like the "Prosperity Camp," whose main topic is the improvement of the believers' financial status and material comfort.

Some Messianic groups prefer to study the Old Covenant, or the Torah, exclusively, and make it their only source of authority, while neglecting the rest of the Scriptures, minimizing their involvement in the Brit Chadashah (New Testament).

I could go on with examples ad nauseam, but I think you get the picture. The point I am trying to make is that the Word of G-d can't be subdivided so that one part stands out above any other. You can find many scriptures to support the Calvinist doctrines. You can also find many to support the Arminian camp. Who is right? In this specific case, I contend that both are right. That might seem like a contradiction to you, but let me explain. You see, the G-d we serve is not illogical; He is supra-logical, as I have mentioned before. That means He is above human logic. He is the G-d who knows the beginning from the end.

Ecclesiastes 3:11says,

> He has made everything appropriate in its time. He has also set eternity in their heart, so that man will not find out **the work which G-d has done from the beginning even to the end.**

And Isaiah 46:9-10 tells us,

> Remember the former things long past, for I am G-d, and there is no other, I am G-d, and there is no one like Me, **declaring the end from the beginning,** and from ancient times things which have not been done, saying, "My purpose will be established, and I will accomplish all for My good pleasure."

In order for Him to be G-d, He must know all things. This would put Him in a category of distinction all by Himself. He also must transcend time and space. He is not trapped by the boundaries of either. He knows all. He is all-powerful. He is everywhere, constantly. He is omniscient, omnipotent, and omnipresent. So how hard would it be for the Lord to know your decision and still be able to grant you free will to make that decision?

This stands in the face of both camps of theology. People find it difficult to let the Lord of all creation be above and beyond their understanding. The Calvinist says that G-d saves those He will save and they have no choice. The Arminian goes to the opposite extreme of the spectrum, and denies G-d the ability to make decisions based on His foreknowledge.

As I said before, all denominations show the dysfunctional nature of the church, because they refuse to see the entire scope of the word from its original Hebrew, or Jewish, context. As a result they find their own little niche or distinctive theology on which to focus. We must break free from this desire to be exclusive and see the whole plan. G-d's Word does not contradict itself, but man's feeble attempt at theology does. In its context, G-d's Word flows without a hitch and exhibits perfect harmony. When we take it out of its Hebraic context, we have problems.

I have spoken to some of my pastoral friends who actually agree with me on these matters. They can't argue with common history. But in response, they say to me things like: "You can't change things overnight"; "You have to feed them with the milk of the Gospel"; "Get them saved first"; "Give them what they know, after that, then you give them more truth." Well, the problem with that thinking is, if you had a baby and found out that the formula you were feeding it was tainted in some way, or not the best for your baby, would you wait for a while before you pulled it from his or her diet? Why would you want to start a new believer on this tainted spiritual food, or continue feeding a more mature believer bad theology? Why feed them something that has no nutrients or is downright detrimental for their growth? When we are instructed to give people milk in the Word, the concept is to give them milk **from the Word**.

Isn't this just like what the Catholic and Protestant churches did when they abandoned the nourishing, prophetic root of the faith for the contrived traditions of a failed system?

We also have to be careful to not think that we can combine good food and bad food together. If we taste good food, and finally realize the benefit of good nourishment, why would we want to slip the bad food back into our diet? If you're serious about good nourishment, then allowing junk food back into your body isn't an option. In the same manner, it seems ridiculous for the church to allow bad doctrines and practices to coexist with truth. G-d certainly didn't endorse it for Israel. Why would He endorse this kind of behavior for the adopted children? Again, we have the problem of men trying to replace the things of G-d with a substitute that has a false foundation.

> Jeremiah 10:1-8 Hear the word which the LORD speaks to you, O house of Israel. Thus says the LORD, **"Do not learn the way of the nations,** and do not be terrified by the signs of the heavens although the nations are terrified by them; **for the customs of the peoples are delusion;** because it is wood cut from the forest, the work of the hands of a craftsman with a cutting tool. They decorate it with silver and with gold; they fasten it with nails and with hammers so that it will not totter. Like a scarecrow in a cucumber field are they, and they cannot speak; they must be carried, because they cannot walk! Do not fear them, for they can do no harm, nor can they do any good." There is none like You, O LORD; You are great, and great is Your name in might. Who would not fear You, O King of the nations? Indeed it is Your due! For among all the wise men of the nations and in all their kingdoms, there is none like You. But they are altogether stupid and foolish in their discipline of delusion—their idol is wood! (Deuteronomy 12:2) **You shall utterly destroy all the places where the nations whom you shall dispossess serve their G-ds,** on the high mountains and on the hills and under every green tree.

> Deuteronomy 16:21 You shall not plant for yourself an Asherah of any kind of tree beside the altar of the LORD your G-d, which you shall make for yourself.

> Jeremiah 2:27 Who says to a tree. "You are my father," and to a stone, "You gave me birth." For they have turned their back to Me, and not their face; but in the time of their trouble they will say, "Arise and save us.'"

> Ezekiel 6:13 Then you will know that I am the LORD, when their slain are among their idols around their altars, on every high hill, on all the tops of the mountains, under every green tree and under every leafy oak—the places where they offered soothing aroma to all their idols.

> Ezekiel 20:27-33 Therefore, son of man, speak to the house of Israel and say to them, 'Thus says the Lord G-D, _Yet in this your fathers have blasphemed Me by acting treacherously against Me. When I had

brought them into the land which I swore to give to them, then they saw every high hill and every leafy tree, and they offered there their sacrifices and there they presented the provocation of their offering. There also they made their soothing aroma and there they poured out their drink offerings.' Then I said to them, 'What is the high place to which you go?' So its name is called Bamah to this day.' Therefore, say to the house of Israel, "Thus says the Lord G-D, **'Will you defile yourselves after the manner of your fathers and play the harlot after their detestable things?** When you offer your gifts, when you cause your sons to pass through the fire, you are defiling yourselves with all your idols to this day. And shall I be inquired of by you, O house of Israel? As I live,' declares the Lord G-D, 'I will not be inquired of by you. What comes into your mind will not come about, when you say: **'We will be like the nations,** like the tribes of the lands, serving wood and stone.' "As I live," declares the Lord G-D, "surely with a mighty hand and with an outstretched arm and with wrath poured out, I shall be king over you."

The Lord wasn't willing to tolerate Israel having any other gods or adopting those gods' customs. Here are few more Scriptures that speak in that same vein:

Leviticus 18:3&30; Leviticus 20:23; Deuteronomy 12:30-31; Ezekiel 20:32; Isaiah 40:19-31, Isaiah 44:9-20, Isaiah 45:20, Isaiah 46:6-8;; Hosea 8:4-6; Habakuk 2:18-19; and Jeremiah 10:8.

It is critical to feed good milk to babies so that they will develop their digestive tracts to eventually receive meat. But while that process of growth happens, they still need proper nourishment to sustain them. The "milk of the Word" that the apostles are talking about is the only Word of G-d they had back then, which was the Tanach, the first, or "Old Testament."

1Peter 2:2 ...like newborn babies, long for the pure milk of the Word, so that by it you may grow in respect to salvation...

Hebrews 5:12-14 For though by this time you ought to be teachers, you have need again for someone to teach you the elementary principles of the oracles of G-d, and you have come to need milk and not solid food. For everyone who partakes only of milk is not accustomed to the word of righteousness, for he is an infant. But solid food is for the mature, who, because of practice, have their senses trained to discern good and evil.

The Law and the Prophets is the only way we know that Yeshua is who He said He was.

Luke. 24:24-27 Some of those who were with us went to the tomb and found it just exactly as the women also had said; but Him they did not see. And He said to them, "O foolish men and slow of heart to believe in all that the prophets have spoken! Was it not necessary for the Mashiach to suffer these things and to enter into His glory?" **Then beginning with Moses and with all the prophets, He explained to them the things concerning Himself in all the Scriptures.**

Luke. 24:44 Now He said to them, "These are My words which I spoke to you while I was still with you, that all things which are written about Me in the Law of Moses and the Prophets and the Psalms must be fulfilled.l

John 1:45 Philip found Nathanael and said to him, **"We have found Him of whom Moses in the Law and also the Prophets wrote –** Yeshua of Nazareth, the son of Joseph."

Acts 26:22-23 So, having obtained help from G-d, I stand to this day testifying both to small and great, **stating nothing but what the Prophets and Moses said was going to take place;** that the Mashiach was to suffer, and that by reason of His resurrection from the dead He would be the first to proclaim light both to the Jewish people and to the Gentiles.

Acts 28:23 When they had set a day for Paul, they came to him at his lodging in large numbers; and he was explaining to them by solemnly testifying about the kingdom of G-d and trying to persuade them concerning Yeshua, from both the Law of Moses and from the Prophets, from morning until evening.

We don't seem to be lacking any proof that Yeshua's message was proclaimed as a Jewish Gospel from a Jewish context to both Jews and Gentiles. It is time for believers to mature, cease imbibing tainted milk, and be nourished on the good milk of

G-d's Word, so that they will be prepared to eat "meat"—the deeper concepts of the Lord's revelation to us in Scripture. Healthy growth only happens through good nourishment. Are congregational leaders too weak as shepherds to give them the correct diet? As shepherds, are we more concerned with the opinion of our sheep than we are for their well-being and growth? Are we willing to give in to their demands for junk food, just because it causes us less stress and aggravation?

I would go as far as to say that all denominations started as a result of this very same behavior. When the "Church" left its family roots and started to preach a "Gospel which was really no Gospel at all," it had to fill the cultural and theological vacuum with a contrived message in an attempt to give meaning and foundation to its faith. The church fathers weren't satisfied with the foundation that G-d gave them because it was from Jewish roots. They despised the original family members, and in their arrogance they assumed that they could replace those original children and have the Father all to themselves.

This is why men like Martin Luther were able to speak so negatively about Jews in the name of his "Christian" faith.

The following are excerpts from the book, **The Jews and Their Lies,** a 65,000-word anti-Semitic treatise written in 1543 by the German Reformation leader Martin Luther:

"I had made up my mind to write no more either about the Jews or against them. But since I learned that these miserable and accursed people do not cease to lure to themselves even us, that is, the Christians, I have published this little book, so that I might be found among those who opposed such poisonous activities of the Jews who warned the Christians to be on their guard against them. I would not have believed that a Christian could be duped by the Jews into taking their exile and wretchedness upon himself. However, the devil is the G-d of the world, and wherever G-d's Word is absent he has an easy task, not only with the weak but also with the strong. May G-d help us. Amen.

The Lord Chose... Who???

What shall we Christians do with this rejected and condemned people, the Jews? Since they live among us, we dare not tolerate their conduct, now that we are aware of their lying and reviling and blaspheming. If we do, we become sharers in their lies, cursing and blasphemy. Thus we cannot extinguish the unquenchable fire of divine wrath, of which the prophets speak, nor can we convert the Jews. With prayer and the fear of G-d we must practice a sharp mercy to see whether we might save at least a few from the glowing flames. We dare not avenge ourselves. Vengeance a thousand times worse than we could wish them already has them by the throat. I shall give you my sincere advice:

First to set fire to their synagogues or schools and to bury and cover with dirt whatever will not burn, so that no man will ever again see a stone or cinder of them. This is to be done in honor of our Lord and of Christendom, so that G-d might see that we are Christians, and do not condone or knowingly tolerate such public lying, cursing, and blaspheming of his Son and of his Christians. For whatever we tolerated in the past unknowingly—and I myself was unaware of it— will be pardoned by G-d. But if we, now that we are informed, were to protect and shield such a house for the Jews, existing right before our very nose, in which they lie about, blaspheme, curse, vilify, and defame Christ and us (as was heard above), it would be the same as if we were doing all this and even worse ourselves, as we very well know."

"Second, I advise that their houses also be razed and destroyed. For they pursue in them the same aims as in their synagogues. Instead they might be lodged under a roof or in a barn, like the gypsies. This will bring home to them that they are not masters in our country, as they boast, but that they are living in exile and in captivity, as they incessantly wail and lament about us before G-d."

"Third, I advise that all their prayer books and Talmudic writings, in which such idolatry, lies, cursing and blasphemy are taught, be taken from them. (remainder omitted)"

"Fourth, I advise that their rabbis be forbidden to teach henceforth on pain of loss of life and limb. For they have justly forfeited the right to such an office by holding the poor Jews captive with the saying of Moses (Deuteronomy 17 [:10 ff.]) in which he commands them to obey their teachers on penalty of death, although Moses clearly adds: "what they teach you in accord with the law of the Lord." Those villains ignore that. They wantonly employ the poor people's obedience contrary to the law of the Lord and infuse them with this poison, cursing, and blasphemy. In the same way the pope also held us captive with the declaration in Matthew 16:18], "You are Peter," etc., inducing us to believe all the lies and deceptions that issued from his devilish mind. He did not teach in accord with the Word of G-d, and therefore he forfeited the right to teach."

"Fifth, I advise that safe conduct on the highways be abolished completely for the Jews. For they have no business in the countryside, since they are not lords, officials, tradesmen, or the like. Let they stay at home. (...remainder omitted)."

"Sixth, I advise that usury be prohibited to them, and that all cash and treasure of silver and gold be taken from them and put aside for safekeeping. The reason for such a measure is that, as said above, they have no other means of earning a livelihood than usury, and by it they have stolen and robbed from us all they possess. Such money should now be used in no other way than the following: Whenever a Jew is sincerely converted, he should be handed one hundred, two hundred, or three hundred florins, as personal circumstances may

suggest. With this he could set himself up in some occupation for the support of his poor wife and children, and the maintenance of the old or feeble. For such evil gains are cursed if they are not put to use with G-d's blessing in a good and worthy cause."

"Seventh, I commend putting a flail, an ax, a hoe, a spade, a distaff, or a spindle into the hands of young, strong Jews and Jewesses and letting them earn their bread in the sweat of their brow, as was imposed on the children of Adam (Gen. 3:19). For it is not fitting that they should let us accursed Goyim toil in the sweat of our faces while they, the holy people, idle away their time behind the stove, feasting and farting, and on top of all, boasting blasphemously of their lordship over the Christians by means of our sweat. No, one should toss out these lazy rogues by the seat of their pants."

In brief, dear princes and lords, those of you who have Jews under your rule if my counsel does not please you, find better advice, so that you and we all can be rid of the unbearable, devilish burden of the Jews, lest we become guilty sharers before G-d in the lies, blasphemy, the defamation, and the curses which the mad Jews indulge in so freely and wantonly against the person of our Lord Jesus Christ, his dear mother, all Christians, all authority, and ourselves. Do not grant them protection, safe conduct, or communion with us.... With this faithful counsel and warning I wish to cleanse and exonerate my conscience.

How can such blatant venom and hate be misconstrued as the message of love and redemption that was preached by Yeshua? How can those who call themselves "Christians" be so blind and not see this as an ungodly lie? This man is called the Father of the Reformation. I cannot see Yeshua, the Jew, endorsing this kind of hateful slander about His very own family.

The "Church" has become very comfortable in what they know. The question is, do they really know what they think they know? I believe that it is necessary to understand the Tanach (Old Testament) in order for us to know the Brit Chadashah (New Testament). This just does not seem like rocket science to me. It surely makes sense that you don't remove a building's foundation from its place once the structure is finished. You then need the foundation even more to gird up the whole structure. Yet, because of this perspective, I am constantly rebuked by my friends and brethren, who say that I am becoming a "Judaizer," one who replaces the theology of salvation by grace with a theology of salvation by works.

"Christians" have for too long been building their faith without a foundation. You can't live a New Covenant life without a First Covenant foundation. When I question my brethren on this matter they get nervous, and cling even more tenaciously to what they think they know, whether it is right or not. When they realize how shaky their foundation really is, they hold on even more to what they have, fearing tearing down what was built and then starting all over again. I compare it to a man who says, "I have set up house, all my pictures are in place, the furniture is comfortable, I'm not moving, no matter what, even if this house falls down." That could be a very dangerous way to live.

At the end of the Sermon on the Mount in Matthew 7:25-29, Yeshua says,

> "Therefore everyone who hears these words of Mine and acts on them, may be compared to a wise man who built his house on the rock. And the rain fell, and the floods came, and the winds blew and slammed against that house; and *yet* it did not fall, for it had been founded on the rock. Everyone who hears these words of Mine and does not act on them, will be like a foolish man who built his house on the sand. The rain fell, and the floods came, and the winds blew and slammed against that house; and it fell—and great was its fall." When Yeshua had finished these words, the crowds were amazed at His teaching; for He was teaching them as one having authority, and not as their scribes.

The Sermon on the Mount needs to be understood in its entirety as one whole body of lessons. You can't separate the things being taught here from the context of the whole sermon; they won't make full sense as the sermon becomes fragmented and disjointed. With that in mind, what are some of the things we are to hear and act upon? After all, He does say that if we do these things, we will be like "a wise man who built his house on the rock."

Building on a rock means we have a firm and safe foundation; to do otherwise would mean complete destruction of our home when a severe storm strikes.

Remember, in the beginning of the sermon, Yeshua said:

> Matthew 5:17-18 Do not think that I came to abolish the Law or the Prophets; I did not come to abolish but to fulfill. For truly I say to you, until heaven and earth pass away, not the smallest letter or stroke shall pass from the Law until all is accomplished.

Understanding this is the key to building our theological foundation. In this statement, Yeshua sets the entire way we are to look at His role as Messiah. His role is not to abolish or abrogate the law, but to fulfill it. This is contrary to what is being taught in most churches today, but it is not inconsistent with, or contrary to Scripture. Yeshua came to build upon the foundation that was already there and finish the house. To fulfill means to make complete. This is where most "Christians" have gone seriously off the mark. They believe Yeshua came to abolish, not to fulfill. We now live in the finished house, not the foundation; but nevertheless, once the house is in place, we don't remove the foundation.

So how does this affect the believer? Does this mean that every law must be kept in order for one to be saved? Absolutely not! What it means is that in order to have a solid structure, the foundation has to be firmly rooted. The celebration of Biblical holidays is not done as a means to salvation but as a memorial and reminder for what has been done to affect that salvation. We celebrate Biblical rituals to memorialize and remember what has been done for us. The alternative is to not do them, and then substitute these prophetic displays with whatever each denomination wants, contrived in the hearts and minds of men.

Does Christmas, with all of its tinsel and hype, really celebrate the prophesied birth of the Messiah? I would be hard pressed to find any Biblical foundational elements in this holiday. **The simple truth is that the Messiah was not born on December 25. Shouldn't the roots of our worship and celebration be from the Scriptures, rather than paganism? The very foundation of the Christmas holiday was birthed in a lie. Yeshua never asked us to celebrate his birth. He also did not ask us to set up a tree in our house and decorate it as a commemoration to His birthday.**

As a matter of fact, Jeremiah 10:1-4 gives us some very specific information against these kinds of practices.

> Hear the word which the LORD speaks to you, O house of Israel. Thus says the LORD, "**Do not learn the way of the nations**, And do not be terrified by the signs of the heavens, although the nations are terrified by them; for **the customs of the peoples are delusion**; because it is wood cut from the forest, the work of the hands of a craftsman with a cutting tool. They decorate *it* with silver and with gold; they fasten it with nails and with hammers so that it will not totter."

Practices of this nature are not new. Why would G-d not tolerate these practices from His people Israel, and yet give "Christians" freedom to do the very thing that repulsed Him? Aren't all believers also His people? Has He changed now that the New Covenant is here?

Sukkot, or Tabernacles, is another time that I clearly see the Messiah. This is a wonderful holiday which represents the forty years that the Lord lived with Israel and provided all their needs while they wandered through the wilderness—G-d dwelling among man. In the millennial kingdom all men will come to Jerusalem and once more celebrate this foundational prophetic event in its final phase of fulfillment, as mentioned in Zechariah 14. During this time men will bring sacrifices to the Lord. These will not be for salvation, but they will be sacrifices of praise and celebration.

The traditional "Christian" would have a problem with this, according to his interpretation. If all of the foundations of the Tanach are to be done away with, then why aren't we celebrating Easter in the millennial kingdom? Again, we have the problem of men trying to replace the things of G-d with a human substitute that has no foundation. Is this what it means to be set free from the law? If destroying the foundation of Biblical prophetic faith is interpreted as "being set free," then I think I'll consider my present state as more desirable than that. At least I know where my faith comes from, and why I believe. My faith is not built on religious cliché and verbiage. My faith is built upon the call of Abraham by the G-d of the universe and His promise to save all mankind through Yeshua. As I said above, we are to live with the Law in our hearts.

> Ezekiel 11:19, 20 And I will give them one heart, and put a new spirit within them. **And I will take the heart of stone out of their flesh and give them a heart of flesh,** that they may walk in My statutes and keep My ordinances and do them. Then they will be My people, and I shall be their G-d.

> Ezekiel 36:24-27 For I will take you from the nations, gather you from all the lands, and bring you into your own land. Then I will sprinkle clean water on you, and you will be clean; I will cleanse you from all your filthiness and from all your idols. **Moreover, I will give you a new heart and put a new spirit within you; and I will re-move the heart of stone from your flesh and give you a heart of**

flesh. I will put My Spirit within you and cause you to walk in My statutes, and you will be careful to observe My ordinances.

We constantly need to be reminded that the Scriptures in Jeremiah 31 say that the law has been put in our hearts. The law has not been abolished; it has been put in its proper place—our hearts (Mt 5:17)—where it was supposed to be since the beginning of our history.

> Jeremiah 31:31 says, "Behold, days are coming," declares the LORD, **"when I will make a new covenant with the house of Israel and with the house of Judah,** not like the covenant which I made with their fathers in the day I took them by the hand to bring them out of the land of Egypt, My covenant which they broke, although I was a husband to them," declares the LORD. **"But this is the covenant which I will make with the house of Israel after those days,"** declares the LORD, **"I will put My law within them and on their heart I will write it; and I will be their G-d, and they shall be My people.** They will not teach again, each man his neighbor and each man his brother, saying, 'Know the LORD,' for they will all know Me, from the least of them to the greatest of them," declares the LORD, "for I will forgive their iniquity, and their sin I will remember no more."

Of course we know we are not saved by the law but by grace (Eph 2:8), like the Gentiles mentioned in Acts 15. But they grew in faith by hearing Moses and the Prophets (Acts 15:19-21). The law now takes its rightful place in the hearts of men because of the work of grace, and we decide to live a life of righteousness as the result of what G-d has done in our lives. We live in relationship to grace, not in obligation to the law. So as Rav Shaul put it, "Should we sin so that grace may abound?" (Rom 6:1). We have to make the distinction between living in grace with the law in our hearts, and living in grace with a lawless attitude. There is a tension here that has to be worked out daily in our lives.

By way of illustration: If a particular man has a problem with driving through intersections with stop signs, this indicates that he disrespects the law. The stop signs were put there to protect society and keep order in our driving habits. The law is not bad. People who break it are bad, or at least they are bad drivers. If a man runs over the stop sign in a drunken stupor, does that mean everyone else is set free from the law, since the sign is down? Considering the state of most cities' public works programs, the sign won't be fixed for some time. If this is the case, then we could never fault the man who ran the stop sign, if he runs through it again. He has been set free from the law. But what about the friendly neighbor who never ran that stop sign in the first place? Does he now have the right to do as he pleases at that intersection? Of course he doesn't! He can't be faulted if the sign is missing; but I have the feeling that, if he was never tempted before, he will continue to stop at that intersection. The reason he stops is not because of a sign or a law. He stops because he is more concerned for the safety of the people in his community than his right to do as he pleases.

The law is in his heart, even though it is not posted. He is a law-keeper, even when there is no law. So for him there is no need for the law, even though he keeps it. He doesn't keep the law to avoid getting a ticket. He keeps it because his heart is right.

So the question we have to ask is this: Who is the one who keeps the law? Is it the one who has been set free from it because it is now in his heart? Or is it the one who is bound by it because it still resides on tablets of stone?

In Romans 2:25-28, Rav Shaul (The Apostle Paul) writes:

For indeed circumcision is of value if you practice the Law, but if you are a transgressor of the Law, your circumcision has become uncircumcision. So if the uncircumcised man keeps the requirements of the Law, will not his uncircumcision be regarded as circumcision? And he who is physically uncircumcised, if he keeps the Law, will he not judge you who though having the letter of the Law and circumcision are a transgressor of the Law? For he is not a Jew who is one outwardly, nor is circumcision that which is outward in the flesh. **But he is a Jew who is one inwardly; and circumcision is that which is of the heart, by the Spirit, not by the letter; and his praise is not from men, but from G-d.**

The word Jew used in this passage comes from the root word Judah which means, "One who praises the Lord." Shaul is using this as a play on words. He is not saying that the Jews are replaced by the uncircumcised Gentiles. What Shaul is saying is that a praiser of God is one who has the praise of the Lord in his heart. His heart has been circumcised. The covenant has been cut into his heart. It makes no difference if the man is a Jew or Gentile. The Lord desires all men to praise Him from the heart. If your flesh is circumcised and your heart is not, then all you have is a mark in your body.

We see in Romans chapter 3 that the issue of Law, works, and grace are reconciled by Rav Shaul.

Romans 3:1-2 Then what advantage has the Jew? Or what is the benefit of circumcision? Great in every respect. First of all, that they were entrusted with the oracles of God.

Rav Shaul first of all reminds us that there is a benefit to being of the physical circumcision in that they were the ones who were given the foundations of faith. If it was not for them the Gentiles would not have come to know the Lord **AT ALL**. They never would have become praisers of the Lord.

Romans 3:3-4 What then? If some did not believe, their unbelief will not nullify the faithfulness of G-d, will it? May it never be! Rather, let

G-d be found true, though every man *be found* a liar, as it is written, **"THAT YOU MAY BE JUSTIFIED IN YOUR WORDS, AND PREVAIL WHEN YOU ARE JUDGED."**

Yet, in spite of all that was given to them, they still don't believe. But the Lord is still faithful. Shaul is setting the theme for the chapter. The problem is with man, not the Lord or His law.

> Romans 3:5-7 But if our unrighteousness demonstrates the righteousness of G-d, what shall we say? The G-d who inflicts wrath is not unrighteous, is He? (I am speaking in human terms.) May it never be! For otherwise, how will G-d judge the world? But if through my lie the truth of G-d abounded to His glory, why am I also still being judged as a sinner?

Shaul now speaks sarcastically to make his point. Considering we are all a total mess and this contrast shows how marvelous the Lord is, then how can He judge us? Our status makes the Lord look good, right? **WRONG!**

> Romans 3:8-9 And why not say (as we are slanderously reported and as some claim that we say), "Let us do evil that good may come"? Their condemnation is just. What then? Are we better than they? Not at all; for we have already charged that both Jews and Greeks are all under sin...

Rav Shaul sets up his argument in this manner to point out that he is not defending sin for any reason whatsoever. All he is trying to do is make it absolutely clear that men are hopelessly lost in comparison to the Lord. Those who accuse them falsely deserve the punishment they get. Everyone, including Jews and Greeks, are all under sin. The rest of his argument follows this pattern; it is men who have failed, not the Law. He backs up all of his theology by quoting many passages from the Tanach to show he is not making this up. This is not a new idea. It is a reoccurring theme throughout the Scriptures.

In the next few verses, Shaul borrows themes from many
Scriptures to paint the picture of our complete failure. Many are
found in Psalms, Proverbs, and Isaiah. (See Psalm 5:9, Psalm
140:3, Psalm 10:7, Proverbs 1:16, Isaiah 59:7, Isaiah 59:8; Psalm
36:1.) Also,

> Romans 3:10-20 ...as it is written, "there is none righteous, not even
> one; there is none who understands, there is none who seeks for
> God, all have turned aside, together they have become useless; there
> is none who does good, there is not even one. Their throat is an open
> grave, with their tongues they keep deceiving. The poison of asps is
> under their lips; whose mouth is full of cursing and bitterness; their
> feet are swift to shed blood, destruction and misery are in their paths,
> and the path of peace they have not known. There is no fear of God
> before their eyes.
> Now we know that whatever the Law says, it speaks to those
> who are under the Law, so that every mouth may be closed and all
> the world may become accountable to God;
> Romans 3:20: ...because by the works of the Law no flesh will
> be justified in His sight; for through the Law comes the knowledge of
> sin.

Does verse 20 mean that Rav Shaul is now advocating lawlessness? Me thinkest not!!

Everyone is under the law because the law shuts the mouth
of all who can't keep it. That is because all have sinned and have
broken the law. Hence, we are all accountable to the Lord for our
actions. We are without excuse. Where there is no law, there is no
knowledge of sin; if there is no knowledge of sin, there is no
understanding of our need; if there is no understanding of our
need, there is no appropriation of grace. The law brought us to
the place where we knew we needed grace.

> Romans 3:21 But now apart from the Law the righteousness of God
> has been manifested, being witnessed by the Law and the Prophets,

Romans 3:22 …even the righteousness of God through faith in Jesus Christ for all those who believe; for there is no distinction;
Romans 3:23: …for all have sinned and fall short of the glory of God,

He is not abolishing the Law; he is helping us to understand it's not fruitful for salvation because we can't keep it. The law does not bring salvation, grace does. This concept was understood by the law and the prophets. All Shaul wants to do is show us our pitiful status so that we will not think we are able to obtain salvation by our own merit. Sin is not an act that we do; it is state of comparison between us and the Lord.

Romans 3:24: …being justified as a gift by His grace through the redemption which is in Yeshua ha Mashiach;

Romans 3:25: …whom God displayed publicly as a propitiation in His blood through faith. *This was* to demonstrate His righteousness, because in the forbearance of God He passed over the sins previously committed;

Romans 3:26: …for the demonstration, *I say,* of His righteousness at the present time, so that He would be just and the justifier of the one who has faith in Yeshua.

Romans 3:27: Where then is boasting? It is excluded. By what kind of law? Of works? No, but by a law of faith.

Romans 3:28: For we maintain that a man is justified by faith apart from works of the Law.

Of course we can't boast because we were unable to keep the Law. This is how we knew our need for grace—because we couldn't fulfill the law. Only Yeshua was able to do that. But the law is not bad, we are. We had to depend on grace. We have faith in the Lord's grace to save us. The law has pointed us to grace.

Romans 3:29: Or is God the God of Jews only? Is He not the God of Gentiles also? Yes, of Gentiles also,

Romans 3:30...since indeed God who will justify the circumcised by faith and the uncircumcised through faith is one.

Romans 3:31 Do we then nullify the Law through faith? May it never be! On the contrary, we establish the Law.

These principles are for Jews and Gentiles because there is only one Lord over all. This law is established for all. Therefore, we don't have the freedom to live lives of lawlessness. Instead we embrace the law, because this is not an indictment against the law, but an indictment against man's sinful nature and his ability to keep the law.

Rav Shaul is not saying that the Law is bad. He is saying we are bad. Why would the Law fail if it was the Lord's perfect will in His Word?

Psalm 119 alone makes reference to the Law of the Lord more times than I have room to write. Each reference is favorable to the Law.

18 Open thou mine eyes, that I may behold wondrous things out of thy law.

29 Remove from me the way of falsehood; and grant me thy law graciously.

34 Give me understanding, and I shall keep thy law; yea, I shall observe it with my whole heart.

44 So shall I observe thy law continually forever and ever.

51 The proud have had me greatly in derision: Yet have I not swerved from thy law.

53 Hot indignation hath taken hold upon me, because of the wicked that forsake thy law.

55 I have remembered thy name, O Jehovah, in the night, and have observed thy law.

61 The cords of the wicked have wrapped me round; but I have not forgotten thy law.

70 Their heart is as fat as grease; but I delight in thy law.

72 The law of thy mouth is better unto me than thousands of gold and silver.

77 Let thy tender mercies come unto me, that I may live; for thy law is my delight.

Thirteen more times in Psalm 119 alone, the Law is mentioned in this favorable light. Do we not think that Rav Shaul understood this? If this is the case, then why on earth would we then think that his writings would reflect contempt for the Law?

Isaiah 2:2-3 teaches us that in the end times the Law would go forth from Zion.

> Now it will come about that in the last days the mountain of the house of the LORD will be established as the chief of the mountains, and will be raised above the hills; and all the nations will stream to it. And many peoples will come and say, "Come, let us go up to the mountain of the LORD, to the house of the God of Jacob; that He may teach us concerning His ways and that we may walk in His paths." **For the law will go forth from Zion and the word of the LORD from Jerusalem.**

Micah chapter 4 echoes the very same sentiment almost word for word.

> Micah 4:1-2 And it will come about in the last days that the mountain of the house of the LORD will be established as the chief of the mountains. It will be raised above the hills, and the peoples will stream to it.
> Many nations will come and say, "Come and let us go up to the mountain of the LORD and to the house of the God of Jacob, that He may teach us about His ways and that we may walk in His paths." **For from Zion will go forth the law, even the word of the LORD from Jerusalem.**

This was the Messianic hope for the Jewish people. The law of the Lord was to be established forever on mount Zion. This time, however, it would reside in the hearts of men. Men's hearts would now be circumcised; they would become true praisers of the Lord. Again, do we not think that Rav Shaul thought of this as he reflected on the hope of Israel and the world? Why would he revile the very promises given to Israel? Why would his writings reflect that kind of sentiment?

As always, I encourage you to read not only the Scriptures that I have quoted in this book, but I expect that you will go to the Word and study them in context for your complete understanding.

Yeshua said this in summary to all of the laws.

Mark 12:28-31: One of the scribes came and heard them arguing, and recognizing that He had answered them well, asked Him, "What commandment is the foremost of all?" Yeshua answered, "The foremost is, **'Hear, O Israel! The Lord our G-d is one Lord; and you shall love the Lord your G-d with all your heart, and with all your soul, and with all your mind, and with all your strength.'** "The second is this, **'You shall love your neighbor as yourself.'** There is no other commandment greater than these."

Keeping the law is only of value if it is in your heart.

Joseph Good writes in his booklet, *Rosh HaShanah and the Messianic Kingdom to Come,* Published by Hatikva Ministries, February 1989:

The Gentile believers of the first century are seldom understood by today"s Biblical scholars. They belonged to a group known as the "sebomenoi," or G-d fearers. These were Gentiles who had left paganism and were already attending synagogues. They observed the Sabbath, as well as the Jewish festivals, and had incorporated into their own life-style many of the Jewish customs. Laws within the Torah defined how they were to be treated as well as how they were to live. It should be pointed out that observance of the Torah had nothing to do with the salvation of an individual, which could only be obtained by faith in the Messiah. For these "sebomenoi" believers, as well as the Jewish believers, the Torah defined their faith and their walk with G-d. Within the Sabbath, festivals, and customs, these two groups understood the working of the Messiah (Colossians 2:16-17). This Torah observance, however, was directly linked to an understanding of the doctrines of the faith.

This is the very sentiment that is found in the Acts 15 scenario. The Jewish believers questioned what they should do with all of the Gentiles who came to faith in the Jewish Messiah.

Acts 15:1 Some men came down from Judea and began teaching the brethren, "Unless you are circumcised according to the custom of Moses, you cannot be saved."

This specifically had to do with the issue of salvation only.

Acts 15:6-7 The apostles and the elders came together to look into this matter. After there had been much debate, Peter stood up and said to them, "Brethren, you know that in the early days G-d made a choice among you, that by my mouth the Gentiles would hear the word of the gospel and believe.

This is what they concluded as a result of their debate:

Acts 15:10-11 Now therefore why do you put G-d to the test by placing upon the neck of the disciples a yoke which neither our fathers nor we have been able to bear? **But we believe that we are saved through the grace of the Lord Yeshua, in the same way as they also are.**

It was pretty conclusive. The Gentiles were saved by grace just like the Jews. There was no need for them to convert to Judaism and become circumcised in order to be saved.

Acts 15:19-21 Therefore it is my judgment that we do not trouble those who are turning to G-d from among the Gentiles, but that we write to them that they abstain from things contaminated by idols and from fornication and from what is strangled and from blood. **For Moses, from ancient generations, has in every city those who preach him, since he is read in the synagogues every Sabbath.**

There were only four things required of them. But just because they were saved by grace, they were not excused from the need to grow in their faith. How that growth took place in their life would be contingent upon their study of the Torah, the Word of G-d. They weren't saved by following the Torah, but they did grow in their faith through study and practice. The only point of reference these G-d-fearing Gentiles had in relationship to the Gospel was a Jewish one, and even though they now understood that salvation was not achieved through the keeping of the Torah, keeping the law was all they knew in order to practice their faith. This happened weekly as they heard the Torah read in the synagogue every Sabbath.

Chapter 10:
The De-Judification of the Gospel, or the "Not -So-Nicea " Council.

Where does all this paganism that has crept into the "Church" come from? No matter how you slice it, every time the Gospel is taken out of its Jewish context, what is left is only a shadow of its original content. Every time you try to replace the original family that the Lord chose with a substitute, you end up with no family at all. This is what the "Church" has been doing for over 1,700 years. It has been Satan's plan to keep the world from salvation. He has done his best to offer a counterfeit plan of salvation, and he has used the "Church" as his tool.

But we must remember that this is not a new problem. As a matter of fact it seems, right from the beginning, there have been those who have wanted to pervert the Gospel and make it something other than that which was taught to us from the beginning. Let's take a brief look at a few of those who have, from the start, tried their best to pervert the Gospel message. We will see how it has affected the "Church" throughout history.

Ignatius of Antioch. 35-107 AD
It is said of him: "Ignatius, bishop of Antioch, one of the Apostolic Fathers. No one connected with the history of the early "Christian Church" is more famous than Ignatius, and yet among the leading churchmen of the time, there is scarcely one about whose career we know so little. Our only trustworthy information

is derived from the letters which he wrote to various churches on his last journey from Antioch to Rome, and from the short epistle of Polycarp to the Philippians."

Yet, this is what he did:

1. He pioneered the Greco-Roman-style based "Christian" religion.
2. He was instrumental in the assimilation of paganism into early "Christianity"
3. He saw the Jewish followers of Yeshua as nothing more than legalists and Judaizers.
4. He despised the observance of the Shabbat.
5. He was in favor of the Ishtar sunrise "Lord's day"
6. He promoted the infallibility of the church.
7. He founded the concept of the universal (Catilupica) church.
8. He believed Mary to be the holy perpetual virgin mother of G-d.

Marcion 110-160 AD

Marcion taught that the G-d of the Old Testament was not the true G-d, but rather that the true and higher G-d had been revealed only with "Jesus Christ." Marcion wrote the *Antitheses* to show the differences between the G-d of the Old Testament and the true G-d.

1. Marcion set out to free the "Church" of false Jewish doctrines.
2. He had an all-Gentile Gospel

3. He believed that only the writings of Paul (Rav Shaul) were inspired.

4. He taught that the G-d of the Old Testament (Tanach) was a ruthless G-d of vengeance, but the G-d of the New Testament (Brit Chadashah) was full of mercy and grace.

5. Marcion coined the terms New and Old Testament.

6. In his day, his all-Gentile church became one of the largest denominations at that time.

7. He was one of the main originators of the Replacement Theology camp.

Tertullian 155-230 AD

Tertullian was a disciple of Montanus, who was a follower of the pagan, mother-goddess of fertility, Sybil. After Montanus became a "Christian," he would fall into a trance and prophesy under the influence of the Holy Ghost. He would insist his utterances were the voice of the Holy Ghost. Tertullian picked up on this practice/anointing, and through demonic possession, coined the phrase, "The Trinity."

These three men have in some way affected all who have called themselves "Christian" for the last 1,800 years or so. They hated the Jewish believers and worked very hard to change the faith of this Jewish Messiah into another Gospel, which was really no Gospel at all.

The first official council of the "Church" was convened by the Roman Emperor Constantine in 325 A.D. This is what was written under his watch in *The Letter Of The Synod In Nicaea To The Egyptians:*

"We also send you the good news of the settlement concerning the holy pasach, namely that in answer to your prayers this question also has been resolved. All the brethren in the East who have hitherto followed the Jewish practice will henceforth observe the custom of the Romans and of yourselves and of all of us who from ancient times have kept Easter together with you. Rejoicing then in these successes and in the common peace and harmony and in the cutting off of all heresy".

In Eusebius' *Life of Constantine, Book III*[1], chapter 18 records Constantine as stating:

"Let us then have nothing in common with the detestable Jewish crowd; for we have received from our Saviour a different way."

As a result of edicts like these, the resurrection was now to be celebrated on the first Sunday after the full moon of the spring equinox. This was done for the purpose of syncretizing the pagan spring fertility rite of Ishtar with the resurrection. This pagan festival celebrated the Mother earth being impregnated by the sun. The "Church" was now to follow a different calculation.

Here are some examples of how the Biblical Holy Days were usurped by men who knew nothing about the Gospel in its Jewish context. These men were leaders in the "Church" of Rome. They were, in essence, pre-Popes before Constantine made Catholicism the state-sanctioned religion.

The following history is from the website, "Archelaos' List of Roman Catholic Popes," *www.archelaos.com/popes/pope.aspx*

Sixtus I (115 to 125) was the first Pope known to have chosen to observe the Last Supper on the Easter day instead of the Passover day. He also ordered that other Roman "**Christians**" do the same which, according to Irenaeus, was in strong opposition with the other churches at the time.

Telesphorus (125 to 136), like his predecessor, Sixtus I, also observed the Last Supper on the Roman Easter day instead of the traditional Jewish Passover day (15th of Nissan).

Pope Pius I (140 to 155) is believed to have officially mandated the observance of the Last Supper on Easter. He is also claimed to have decreed various forms of punishments of penance to priests who dropped or spilled the bread or wine.

Pope Anicetus (155 to 166) argued with the other bishops over the importance of sacrificing the Passover day in order to gain greater favor with the Emperor for the sake of Christianity.

It was attributed to Pope Soter (166 to 175) that the "Christian" Passover should never coincide with the Jewish observance. During the time of the Roman Emperor Constantine, this change became official. The "Christian' festival would now be independent of the Bible's Hebrew calendar. By 325 A.D., Constantine settled the issue by officially decreeing that the Last Supper should be observed on Easter and forbade anyone from observing it on Passover.

Who gave these men the authority to uproot festivals from the Scriptures? This is where the official divorce of the Gospel from its Jewish roots happened. Once it was no longer a Jewish message, it could change and become anything. From that point on, the truth of the Gospel was lost, the children of Abraham were dispossessed of their role as being a light to the Gentiles, and Yeshua became a "Catholic"—or at least, a non-Jew.

The Catholic Church says they receive their authority from the call of Peter in Matthew 16:13-20

Now when Yeshua came into the district of Caesarea Philippi, He was asking His disciples, "Who do people say that the Son of Man is?" And they said, "Some *say* John the Baptist; and others, Elijah; but still others, Jeremiah, or one of the prophets." He said to them, "But who do you say that I am?" Simon Peter answered, "You are the Mashiach, the Son of the living God." And Yeshua said to him, —Blessed are you, Simon Barjona, because flesh and blood did not

reveal this to you, but My Father who is in heaven. "I also say to you
that you are Peter, and upon this rock I will build My church; and the
gates of Hades will not overpower it. "I will give you the keys of the
kingdom of heaven; and whatever you bind on earth shall have been
bound in heaven, and whatever you loose on earth shall have been
loosed in heaven." Then He warned the disciples that they should tell
no one that He was the Moshiach.

They base their doctrine of papal succession from this statement. In that doctrine they believe that Peter was ordained the
leader of the "New Church" as the first Pope. They also believe
that they, "The Catholic Church," are the recipients of that
succession through the establishment of the Papal system.

Pope Innocent III (1160 to1216) said, "The successor of Peter is the Vicar of Christ; he has been established as a mediator
between God and man—below God but beyond man; less than
God but more than man—who shall judge all and be judged by
no one."

It makes absolutely no sense to believe that the Lord ordained through Peter, this Jewish man who at one time refused to
eat with Gentiles (Gal 2:11-14), a Papal system and "Church" that
would lead the way throughout the centuries that would be so
totally anti-Semitic. Why would the Lord put His stamp of
approval on a system like that? How can one believe that the
Lord would endorse this Catholic succession of Papal authority
through Peter? Did Peter envision this as a means of evangelizing
the world—by killing all who opposed his successors, especially
his brethren?

This divorce was not totally to be blamed on the "Christians"
though, because the Jews also abdicated from their G-d-given job
description and turned it over to the Gentiles. This means all men
have failed the Lord again. Just like the prodigal son, the Jewish

people left their estate. After they left, the adopted children felt that they now had the right to usurp the natural-born children. This is where the problem lies, and it continues on the same course even today.

The Holy Days celebrated by the Jews were meant to be prophetic displays of the Messiah to come. We must remember that we were told by G-d that these were His appointed times and seasons—His "moadim."

> The LORD spoke again to Moses, saying, "Speak to the sons of Israel and say to them, „The **LORD"S appointed times which you shall proclaim as holy convocations—My appointed times are these:…**‴(Leviticus 23:1-2)

I said it before and I will say it again: I think that keeping appointments with G-d is a pretty important thing to do. I know that I wouldn't want to miss one.

Let me give you a few more examples of critical appointments that were given by the Lord, pointing us to the coming of the Messiah. The Passover lamb was to be chosen on the 10th day of Nissan, the first month of the religious calendar year. This is the day on which Yeshua was hailed as king during His triumphal entry into Jerusalem.

> John 12:12-15: On the next day the large crowd who had come to the feast, when they heard that Yeshua was coming to Jerusalem, took the branches of the palm trees and went out to meet Him, and began to shout, "Hosanna! Blessed is he who comes in the name of the lord, even the King of Israel." Yeshua, finding a young donkey, sat on it; as it is written, "Fear not, daughter of Zion; behold, your king is coming, seated on a donkey's colt."

The above-mentioned feast was Passover. The day of preparation for the Passover Lamb was the 14th of Nissan. This was the day that the Passover lamb was to be sacrificed. This was also the day that Yeshua was crucified.

The First Fruits offering was made three days later to begin the counting of the Omer. This is the day that Yeshua arose from the dead. He was the first fruits of the resurrection from the dead.

1 Corinthians 15:20 "But now Mashiach has been raised from the dead, the first fruits of those who are asleep."

If you take the resurrection out of its original context of the time and history of the Passover Feast, then Yeshua is not the Passover lamb sacrificed from the foundation of the world. This is what we miss by not keeping this appointment with G-d.

1 Corinthians 5:7 says, "Clean out the old leaven so that you may be a new lump, just as you are in fact unleavened. For Mashiach our Passover also has been sacrificed."

People who call themselves believers all over the world continue to minimize the importance of this appointment with the Lord, and substitute it with meaningless pagan rituals year after year. Why is this so? I contend it is because they first despised—and later completely forgot—the family into which they entered when they became the spiritual seed of Abraham. Therefore, the important family celebrations are now negated, substituted, and invalidated. The excuse they use to justify their negation of the Biblical Holy Days is to say that celebrating them would constitute going back to the law. To use a modern analogy: Do we celebrate our wedding anniversaries because we are obligated by law, or do we celebrate because it is important to commemorate the sacred commitment that we made on that day?

A young woman and her family left my congregation because she claimed all I ever did was talk about Israel. Ironically, she came to the congregation because she was tired of the "Church's" practice of ignoring Israel. I asked her how could I do anything but what I was doing. The entire Tanach, two thirds of the Scriptures, deals exclusively with Israel in the context of its relationship to the Lord and to the rest of the world (i.e. the Gentiles). The entire Brit Chadashah, the New Testament, deals with the fulfillment of this relationship. What else should I talk about when teaching the Word of the Lord? If I ignore G-d's original family, I have nothing which to bring the Gentiles into. Studying Israel's history shows me that, as G-d was faithful to keep His promises to His covenant people, so He will be faithful to you and me.

Chapter 11:
What About the Canaanites?

Some might ask the question: What about the tribes that the Lord commanded the Israelites to drive out of the land? After all, He did command Israel to dispossess the "indigenous" people from the land that they were occupying.

> Deuteronomy 11:22-23 For if you are careful to keep all this commandment which I am commanding you to do, to love the LORD your G-d, to walk in all His ways and hold fast to Him, **then the LORD will drive out all these nations from before you, and you will dispossess nations greater and mightier than you.**

This does not seem to be consistent with a plan to save the world through the Jews. Why would the G-d of Israel want to do such a thing to the people He wanted to save? This is the $50,000 question. I have even heard some suggest that the G-d of the Old Testament is a harsh G-d of vengeance and war, while the G-d of the New Testament is a Lord of grace, love, and peace. This kind of statement would seem to indicate that either there are two G-ds, or that the Lord changed His nature when the New Covenant was entered into.

Not only is this not true, but the lie again is perpetuated because of the lack of scriptural perspective from a Jewish context. In order to understand what the Lord's plan and motivation for that plan was, we need to see it as it unfolded in the Scriptures. So let's start from the beginning and follow it through till the end.

The first reference to driving out the nations is found in Exodus 23:23-24:

> For My angel will go before you and bring you in to the land of the Amorites, the Hittites, the Perizzites, the Canaanites, the Hivites and the Jebusites; and I will completely destroy them. **You shall not worship their gods, nor serve them, nor do according to their deeds; but you shall utterly overthrow them and break their sacred pillars in pieces.**

The question we have to ask first is: Who were these people, and what were the deeds that the G-d of Israel was talking about? In other passages, the Lord warns the children of Israel to have nothing to do with the "customs or practices" of these nations.

> Leviticus 20:22-24 You are therefore to keep all My statutes and all My ordinances and do them, so that the land to which I am bringing you to live will not spew you out. **Moreover, you shall not follow the customs of the nation which I will drive out before you, for they did all these things, and therefore I have abhorred them.** Hence I have said to you, "You are to possess their land, and I, Myself, will give it to you to possess it, a land flowing with milk and honey. I am the LORD your G-d, who has separated you from the peoples."

> Numbers 33:50-53 Then the LORD spoke to Moses in the plains of Moab by the Jordan opposite Jericho, saying, "Speak to the sons of Israel and say to them, 'When you cross over the Jordan into the land of Canaan, then **you shall drive out all the inhabitants of the land from before you, and destroy all their figured stones, and destroy all their molten images, and demolish all their high places; and you shall take possession of the land and live in it, for I have given the land to you to possess it.'"**

If we examine the issue historically, we can see who these foreign nations were and what they practiced that was so detestable to the Lord. In Numbers 21, we read about the Israelites' conflict with a nation known as the Amorites.

> Numbers 21:21-25 Then Israel sent messengers to Sihon, king of the Amorites, saying, "Let me pass through your land. **We will not turn**

off into field or vineyard; we will not drink water from wells. We will go by the king's highway until we have passed through your border." But Sihon would not permit Israel to pass through his border. So Sihon gathered all his people and went out against Israel in the wilderness, and came to Jahaz and fought against Israel. Then Israel struck him with the edge of the sword, and took possession of his land from the Arnon to the Jabbok, as far as the sons of Ammon; for the border of the sons of Ammon was Jazer. Israel took all these cities and Israel lived in all the cities of the Amorites, in Heshbon, and in all her villages.

The children of Israel, while making their way through the land of the Amorites and on their way to the Promised Land, offered to stay on the established way and not turn to the right or the left. They also agreed not to use any of the resources of the land. Their only request to Sihon, the king, was that he should let them pass uninterrupted. This he would not let them do. Not only would he not let them pass, he declared war against the children of Israel.

We have to remember that the children of Israel were doing their best to just survive as a people after they left slavery in Egypt. Their only other option was to lie down and die. The graciousness in their offer to Sihon surely shows the intent of their heart. The Lord reminded them that, previous to their entering the land, they were to treat the stranger with equity and justice.

Exodus 22:21: You shall not wrong a stranger or oppress him, for you were strangers in the land of Egypt.

Exodus 23:9: You shall not oppress a stranger, since you yourselves know the feelings of a stranger, for you also were strangers in the land of Egypt.

I would like to propose that the wars Israel fought in the name of the Lord against the "indigenous peoples" were in self-defense only. We see this repeatedly.

The seven nations that were to be dispossessed were the Hittites, Girgashites, Amorites, Canaanites, Perizzites, the Hivites and the Jebusites, Just who were these nations? These are the meanings of their names: Hittites: Sons of Terror; Girgashites: Clay dwellers; Amorites: Mountain people, renowned; Canaanites: Lowlands people; Perizzites: Belonging to a village; Hivites: Villagers; Jebusites: Threshers.

The descendants of Noah's grandson, Canaan, took possession of this land, except for Philistia. Canaan himself had eleven sons, and each bore a tribe. Six of them dwelt in Syria and Phoenicia, and the remaining five in Canaan. The Lord mentioned seven nations by name which inhabited the land of Canaan from the time of Abraham until the time of Joshua.

For the sake of time, I will give a brief synopsis of some of their detestable practices. We do not have an abundance of information on these people, probably because most of them have not existed for the last 3,000 years.

In the Book of Ezra, we see that the children of Israel grieved the Lord by engaging in detestable practices against which He had warned them.

> Ezra 9:1-2 Now when these things had been completed, the princes approached me, saying, **"The people of Israel and the priests and the Levites have not separated themselves from the peoples of the lands, according to their abominations,** those of the Canaanites, the Hittites, the Perizzites, the Jebusites, the Ammonites, the Moabites, the Egyptians and the Amorites. For they have taken some of their daughters as wives for themselves and for their sons, so that **the holy race has intermingled with the peoples of the lands;**

indeed, the hands of the princes and the rulers have been foremost in this unfaithfulness."

So nu, what did they do already?

First of all, they tried to destroy the children of Israel.

No Ammonite or Moabite shall enter the assembly of the LORD; none of their descendants, even to the tenth generation, shall ever enter the assembly of the Lord, because they did not meet you with food and water on the way when you came out of Egypt, and because they hired against you Balaam the son of Beor from Pethor of Mesopotamia, to curse you. (Deuteronomy 23:3-4)

Second, they tempted the children of Israel to worship other gods and betray their own Lord.

Numbers 25:1-3 While Israel remained at Shittim, the people began to play the harlot with the daughters of Moab. For they invited the people to the sacrifices of their gods, and the people ate and bowed down to their gods. So Israel joined themselves to Baal of Peor, and the LORD was angry against Israel.

Third, they taught the children of Israel to burn their very own sons and daughters as a sacrifice to their false gods.

Deuteronomy 12:29-31 When the LORD your G-d cuts off before you the nations which you are going in to dispossess, and you dispossess them and dwell in their land, beware that you are not ensnared to follow them, after they are destroyed before you, and that you *do not inquire after their gods*, saying, 'How do these nations serve their G-ds, that I also may do likewise?' **You shall not behave thus toward the LORD your G-d**, for every abominable act which the LORD hates they have done for their gods; **for they even burn their sons and daughters in the fire to their G-ds.**

This refers to imitating the practices of the pagans. The Lord did not give us permission to sanctify pagan practices, or use them as a template to worship Him. The horrific practice of offering human sacrifices existed universally among ancient nations, like the Phoenicians and Carthaginians. They were descendants from the Canaanite nations, and they had the custom of sacrificing their children to Moloch or Saturn.

Fourth, the children of Israel were tempted to play the harlot and pollute themselves with all manner of sexual perversions.

> Hosea 4:14 I will not punish your daughters when they play the harlot or your brides when they commit adultery, for the men themselves go apart with harlots and offer sacrifices with temple prostitutes; so the people without understanding are ruined.

> 1Kings 14:22-24 Judah did evil in the sight of the LORD, and they provoked Him to jealousy more than all that their fathers had done, with the sins which they committed. For they also built for themselves high places and sacred pillars and Asherim on every high hill and beneath every luxuriant tree. There were also male cult prostitutes in the land. They did according to all the abominations of the nations which the LORD dispossessed before the sons of Israel.

It is scripturally very clear that the Lord instructed the children of Israel how they were to relate to the nations in the land that they were to inherit. They were to avoid having anything to do with any of their practices. There is no room for the imagination or reinterpretation of what the Lord said. Here are just a few references:

> Numbers 33:50-56 Then the LORD spoke to Moses in the plains of Moab by the Jordan opposite Jericho, saying, "Speak to the sons of Israel and say to them, 'When you cross over the Jordan into the land of Canaan, then you shall drive out all the inhabitants of the land from before you, and **destroy all their figured stones, and destroy all their molten images and demolish all their high places**; and you shall take possession of the land and live in it, for I have given the land to you to possess it. You shall inherit the land by lot according to your families; to the larger you shall give more inheritance, and to the smaller you shall give less inheritance. Wherever the lot falls to anyone that shall be his. You shall inherit according to the tribes of your fathers.
> But if you do not drive out the inhabitants of the land from before you, then it shall come about that those whom you let remain of them will become as pricks in your eyes and as thorns in your sides,

and they will trouble you in the land in which you live. And as I plan to do to them, so I will do to you."

Deuteronomy 12:1-7 These are the statutes and the judgments which you shall carefully observe in the land which the LORD, the G-d of your fathers, has given you to possess as long as you live on the earth. **You shall utterly destroy all the places where the nations whom you shall dispossess serve their gods, on the high mountains and on the hills and under every green tree. You shall tear down their altars and smash their sacred pillars and burn their Asherim with fire, and you shall cut down the engraved images of their gods and obliterate their name from that place.** You shall not act like this toward the LORD your G-d. But **you shall seek the LORD at the place which the LORD your G-d will choose form all your tribes, to establish His name there for His dwelling, and there you shall come. There you shall bring your burnt offerings, your sacrifices, your tithes,** the contribution of your hand, your votive offerings, your freewill offerings, and the firstborn of your herd and of your flock. There also you and your households shall eat before the LORD your G-d, and rejoice in all your undertakings in which the LORD your G-d has blessed you.

Deuteronomy 12:29-32 When the LORD your G-d cuts off before you the nations which you are going in to dispossess, and you dispossess them and dwell in their land, **beware that you are not ensnared to follow them, after they are destroyed before you, and that you do not inquire after their gods, saying, "How do these nations serve their gods, that I also may do likewise?"** You shall not behave thus toward the LORD your G-d, for every abominable act which the LORD hates they have done for their gods; for they even burn their sons and daughters in the fire to their gods. Whatever I command you, you shall be careful to do; you shall not add to nor take away from it.

We see that the Lord wanted the children of Israel to keep themselves totally separate from pagan customs and rituals. They were not to combine, share, or copy pagan worship in any manner. The reason was because He had a place which He would designate for His true worship. This would be the Temple in Jerusalem, as Moses said:

Deuteronomy 12:5-6 But you shall seek the LORD at the place which the LORD your G-d will choose from all your tribes, to establish His name there for His dwelling, and there you shall come. There you shall bring your burnt offerings, your sacrifices, your tithes...

The Lord had already chosen a place where He would establish His name. No other place would do. The reason was that in this place He would set up a system that would be prophetic of His Messiah (Anointed One) to come in the future. The Lord will not share His glory with another.

Isaiah 42:8 "I am the LORD, that is My name; I will not give My glory to another, nor My praise to graven images."

Israel's very survival as a people was dependent upon the removal of any influences that would take them away from their Lord and divide them as a people. If Israel didn't survive, then the Messiah would not have been born. If Yeshua had not been born, then the Gentiles would not have been brought into the family. It was not an act of barbarity to have Israel dispossess these people from the land, it was an act of mercy for the rest of the world.

We also need to take into consideration that the Lord did not judge only the pagan world. He held Israel to a higher standard, and judged them before He did any other people. When Israel fell into sin, they were dealt with just as severely, if not more so, than anyone else. This one factor alone assures us that the G-d of Israel is just. Everything He does is for the benefit of mankind, the free-will agents He created. We are volitional beings, and the Lord will not violate that freedom. But neither will He allow all that He has created to be polluted by our corrupt moral choices.

Henry M. Morse

This is why the children of Israel were not to combine the Lord's celebrations with any other celebration dedicated to a false god. This is what got the kings of Israel in trouble with the Lord, and they were judged harshly for it. Such was the case with Jeroboam and Rehoboam.

1 Kings 12:26-33 Jeroboam said in his heart, "Now the kingdom will return to the house of David. If this people go up to offer sacrifices in the house of the LORD at Jerusalem, then the heart of this people will return to their lord, even to Rehoboam, king of Judah; and they will kill me and return to Rehoboam, king of Judah." So the king consulted, and made two golden calves, and he said to them, "It is too much for you to go up to Jerusalem; behold your gods, O Israel, that brought you up from the land of Egypt. He set one in Bethel, and the other he put in Dan. **Now this thing became a sin, for the people went to worship before the one as far as Dan. And he made houses on high places, and made priests from among all the people who were not of the sons of Levi. Jeroboam instituted a feast in the eighth month on the fifteenth day of the month, like the feast which is in Judah, and he went up to the altar; thus he did in Bethel, sacrificing to the calves which he had made. And he stationed in Bethel the priests of the high places which he had made.** Then he went up to the altar which he had made in Bethel on the fifteenth day in the eighth month, even in the month which he had devised in his own heart; and he instituted a feast for the sons of Israel and went up to the altar to burn incense. Jeroboam of the Northern kingdom was determined to do all that he could to replace the Temple feasts, the priests, and eventually the G-d of Jacob with totally invented man-made substitutes. Even Judah, the Southern Kingdom, after the death of Rehoboam, fell into sin and eventually committed the same sin of worshiping in the high places.

1 Kings 14:21-24 Now Rehoboam, the son of Solomon, reigned in Judah. Rehoboam was forty-one years old when he became king, and he reigned seventeen years in Jerusalem, the city which the LORD had chosen from all the tribes of Israel to put His name there. And his mother's name was Naamah the Ammonitess. **Judah did evil in the sight of the LORD, and they provoked Him to jealousy more than all that their fathers had done, with the sins which they committed. For they also built for themselves high places**

125

and sacred pillars and Asherim on every high hill and beneath every luxuriant tree. There were also male cult prostitutes in the land. They did according to all the abominations of the nations which the LORD dispossessed before the sons of Israel.

These "high places" were substitutes for the real place that the Lord wanted the children of Israel to worship. Israel was to have nothing to do with the substitute. These places were defiled with human sacrifice and sexual practices committed in dedication to their false gods. The Lord was not willing to share His glory with anyone—period! No exceptions!

> 1 Kings 22:41-43 Now Jehoshaphat, the son of Asa, became king over Judah in the fourth year of Ahab, king of Israel. Jehoshaphat was thirty-five years old when he became king, and he reigned twenty-five years in Jerusalem. And his mother's name was Azubah the daughter of Shilhi. He walked in all the way of Asa his father; he did not turn aside from it, doing right in the sight of the LORD. **However, the high places were not taken away; the people still sacrificed and burnt incense on the high places.**

Even though Jehoshaphat of Judah did some very good things, the one thing he failed to do was to tear down the high places—the same failing as Jehoash.

> 2 Kings 12:1-3: In the seventh year of Jehu, Jehoash became king, and he reigned forty years in Jerusalem; and his mother's name was Zibiah of Beersheba. Jehoash did right in the sight of the LORD all his days in which Jehoiada the priest instructed him. **Only the high places were not taken away; the people still sacrificed and burned incense on the high places.**

There was just no wiggle-room. The Lord wanted those high places torn down. Those were the places dedicated to the heinous practices of the pagans. The children of Israel just wouldn't do it. The "Church" does the same thing, and yet they refuse to see the parallel. Christmas, Easter, Good Friday, Lent, Ashe Wednesday, Maundy Thursday, Valentine's Day, etc., are all substitutes for the real Biblical events that were meant to be prophetic displays of the coming Messiah.

The Christmas hollow day has its roots totally in paganism, as does Easter. The practices of the "Catholic Church" were polluted because they syncretized pagan rituals with Biblical faith, thus polluting the Word of the Lord. Well, whether you want to accept it or not, the same issue stands for the rest of their contrived hollow days. Christmas and Easter both have their roots in a failed pagan system. Let me point out just a few of the customs and their origins.

The date of December 25 probably originated with the ancient "birthday" of the sun god, Mithra, a pagan deity whose religious influence became widespread in the Roman Empire during the first few centuries A.D. Mithra was related to the Semitic sun god, Shamash, and his worship spread throughout Asia to Europe where he was called Deus Sol Invictus Mithras. Rome was well-known for absorbing the pagan religions and rituals of its widespread empire. As such, Rome converted this pagan legacy to a celebration of the god, Saturn, and the rebirth of the sun god during the winter solstice period. The winter holiday became known as Saturnalia and began the week prior to December 25. The festival was characterized by gift-giving, feasting, singing and downright debauchery, as the priests of Saturn carried wreaths of evergreen boughs in procession throughout the Roman temples.[3]

Variations of this pagan holiday flourished throughout the first few centuries after Jesus Christ, but it probably wasn't until 336 A.D. that Emperor Constantine officially converted this pagan tradition into the "Christian" holiday of "Christmas."

Again, the reason why this is so grievous to the Lord is because of what He said in His Word about His appointed times and seasons.

Leviticus 23:1-2 The Lord spoke again to Moses, saying, "Speak to the sons of Israel and say to them, 'The Lord's appointed times which

3 www.origin-of-Christmas.com

you shall proclaim as holy convocations—My appointed times are these:...'"

Lev 23:44 So Moses declared to the sons of Israel the appointed times of the LORD.

Substitutes are the trick of the enemy. Satan has tried to give us a substitute for everything the Lord has given us.

We have replaced Sukkot, the Holy Day that represents Adonai (the Lord) dwelling among man for forty years in the wilderness, with Christmas. We have substituted the real for the contrived. Is there any difference between this and the practices of the children of Israel mentioned in the scriptures above? If we were supposed to celebrate Christmas and Easter, then why aren't we going to celebrate them in the millennial kingdom? Admittedly, I find it very curious that we are going to celebrate Sukkot (the Feast of Booths) in the Millennium.

> Zechariah 14:2-4 For I will gather all the nations against Jerusalem to battle, and the city will be captured, the houses plundered, the women ravished and half of the city exiled, but the rest of the people will not be cut off from the city. Then the LORD will go forth and fight against those nations, as when He fights on a day of battle. In that day His feet will stand on the Mount of Olives, which is in front of Jerusalem on the east; and the Mount of Olives will be split in its middle from east to west by a very large valley, so that half of the mountain will move toward the north and the other half toward the south.

> Zechariah 14:9 And the LORD will be king over all the earth; in that day the LORD will be the only one, and His name the only one.

> Zechariah 14:16 Then it will come about that any who are left of all the nations that went against Jerusalem will go up from year to year to worship the King, the LORD of hosts, and to **celebrate the Feast of Booths**.

The Scriptures clearly declare that there is a right and wrong way to celebrate and worship. The Lord prescribed the acceptable and right way, and only He reserved the right to do so. Now that you have the truth, you will have to ask yourself the question: How will you deal with these contrived, pagan-derived hollow days? Will they be your substitutes for the real Biblical celebrations? Will they be your high places?

Smith"s Bible Dictionary defines the High Places:
High Places. *(Hebrew,* **bamoth***). From the top of Hermon to the crest of the low hills, all over the land, there are evidences that they were used for religious rites, both in idolatrous and in pure worship. The Temple on Moriah was intended to supersede all other high places, and no other worship was allowed, except on special occasions.*

Easton"s Dictionary of the Bible:
High Place. *An eminence, natural or artificial, where worship by sacrifice or offerings was made (1Kings 13:32; 2Kings 17:29). The first altar after the Flood was built on a mountain (Gen.8:20). Abraham also built an altar on a mountain (Gen.12:7-8). It was on a mountain in Gilead that Laban and Jacob offered sacrifices (Gen.31:54). After the Israelites entered the Promised Land they were strictly enjoined to overthrow the high places of the Canaanites (Exod.34:13; Deut.7:5; Deut.12:2; Deut.12:3), and they were forbidden to worship the Lord on high places (Deut.12:11-14), and were enjoined to use but one altar for sacrifices (Lev.17:3-4; Deut.16:21). However, the injunction against high places was very imperfectly obeyed, and we find repeated negative mention made of them (2Kings 14:4; 15:4, 35; 2Chron.15:17, etc.).*

There seems to be a very simple theme here. The Lord wasn't going to tolerate any form of worship that wasn't prescribed by Him. This was the reason the children of Israel had to dispossess the other nations. If they allowed the idolatrous nations to remain, then knowledge of the one, true G-d would have been deeply compromised. If the Lord does not have the right to judge the wicked, then no one does.

For centuries men have brought down oppressive regimes in battle to liberate the oppressed. This was the case in World War II; the Allies liberated Europe from the Nazis. No man in his right mind would declare that this was not needed. Countless scores of innocent people died in that war. But we believed in a greater good for mankind and fought in judgment against fascism and oppression of mankind. I contend that this is also what the Lord did. He desired the greater good for mankind and eliminated nations that were bent on the moral destruction of the world. Israel was the nation He used as His agent of justice against those evil nations.

I am not writing these things in judgment of anyone's salvation. Of course we know we are not saved because we celebrate the holy days. This is not a salvation issue, although it could become one, depending upon the reader's condition of his heart. Once we know the truth, will we continue in a lie? Will we maintain false religious rituals just because we have done them all of our lives?

Preaching is a Biblical mandate, just like baptism. As Rav Shaul (The Apostle Paul) wrote:

> 1Corinthians 1:17 **For Mashiach did not send me to baptize, but to preach the gospel**, not in cleverness of speech, so that the cross of Mashiach would not be made void.

We know that we are not saved through baptism, yet we are commanded to participate in it; so too with preaching Biblical truth.

What I am doing here is defending the integrity of Yeshua's incarnation and resurrection by showing their fulfillment in the Biblical holy days—the moadim, (appointed times and seasons)—as opposed to their pagan counterparts, the Canaanites in our lives. These Biblical moadim were given to the first family of the Lord as symbols and memorials of His relationship with them. I am speaking against those who stand opposed to the Scriptures by using adopted pagan practices as a template to worship the one true G-d. The truth of G-d's Word should and must be greater in our lives than the traditions of men.

This is why Yeshua rebuked the Pharisees and Sadducees in Matthew 23. They were more concerned with fulfilling the traditions of men than the Word of the Lord.

Chapter 12:
So Who Needs Salvation?

We have dealt with the role and calling of the Jewish people in detail. We have declared, without any hesitation, that the Jewish people were called to be a light to the Gentiles (Or la Goyim). This means that the light which the Jews bring to the nations is the knowledge of the Lord, so that the entire world might have a relationship with Him.

In other words, salvation is what is described in Isaiah 42:6:

I, Jehovah, have called thee in righteousness, and will hold thy hand, and will keep thee, and give thee for a covenant of the people, for a light of the Gentiles;

And in Isaiah 49:6:

"Yea", he saith, "It is too light a thing that thou shouldest be my servant to raise up the tribes of Jacob, and to restore the preserved of Israel: I will also give thee for a light to the Gentiles, that thou mayest be my salvation unto the end of the earth."

This mandates that we have to define salvation in detail, so that there will be no confusion as to what that means.

The word salvation carries so much unnecessary baggage because of the "Christian" application to it. That being said, I will be very careful to avoid the cliché of the white Anglo-Saxon, American-Protestant entrepreneurial, capitalistic version of the Gospel.

The Hebrew word "Yeshua" carries much broader and deeper nuances than the way it is translated and used as "salvation" in "Christian" culture and theology. Salvation for the early Hebrew meant deliverance from slavery in Egypt, the redemption of the first born from the Angel of Death. The crossing of the Red Sea described in Exodus 14:3 was a type of salvation from the pursuit of Pharaoh. The holy days were also foreshadows of salvation. Yom Kippur deals with forgiveness and salvation from our sins through the sacrifices. Purim details our deliverance and salvation from the threat of total annihilation by the hand of Haman. Sukkot shows us that the Lord's provision and saving grace was with us while we were in the wilderness. All of these events, and many, many more, were foreshadows and types of the salvation that was to finally come when the Mashiach would appear.

The word salvation in Hebrew is literally "Yeshua" and it means... *something saved, that is, (abstractly) deliverance; hence aid, victory, prosperity: - deliverance, health, help (-ing), salvation, save, saving (health), welfare.* The word is found 111 times in the Tenach.

There are also other forms of the word used.

yesha ' *liberty, deliverance, prosperity: - safety, salvation, saving.*

tesh-oo-ah', *rescue (literally or figuratively, personal, national or spiritual): - deliverance, help, safety, salvation, victory.*

No matter how it is used, it connotes deliverance and all the good that follows it. The question that needs to be asked is: Does this salvation only apply to the physical world, or is there a spiritual application as well?

The first time it is used is in Genesis 49:18, "For Your salvation I wait, O LORD." This is where Jacob gathers his twelve sons to tell them of their fate and the fate of their progeny." This passage is in reference to the tribe of Dan. Other books of the Bible that use this word are Psalms and Isaiah, where this word is used most often. So I will use references from those books to see how it is applied in different contexts.

Psalm 3:8: **Salvation** belongs to the LORD; Your blessing be upon Your people! Selah.

Psalm 9:14: That I may tell of all Your praises, that in the gates of the daughter of Zion I may rejoice in Your **salvation**.

Psalm 37:39: But the **salvation** of the righteous is from the LORD; He is their strength in time of trouble.

Isaiah 62:1: For Zion's sake I will not keep silent, and for Jerusalem's sake I will not keep quiet, until her righteousness goes forth like brightness, and her **salvation** like a torch that is burning.

Isaiah 61:10: I will rejoice greatly in the LORD, my soul will exult in my G-d; for He has clothed me with garments of **salvation**, He has wrapped me with a robe of righteousness, as a bridegroom decks himself with a garland, and as a bride adorns herself with her jewels.

Isaiah 12:2: Behold, G-d is my **salvation**, I will trust and not be afraid; for the LORD G-D is my strength and song, and He has become my **salvation**.

Isaiah 49:6: He says, "It is too small a thing that You should be My servant to raise up the tribes of Jacob and to restore the preserved ones of Israel; I will also make You a light of the nations so that My **salvation** may reach to the end of the earth."

David, in his writing of the Psalms, seems to be more concerned with the physical aspect of deliverance in regards to salvation. Yet Isaiah's understanding of salvation extends way beyond just physical deliverance; salvation for him has its focus on spiritual deliverance. This salvation also extends to the Gentiles. Either way, it is used in both contexts to ask for physical and spiritual salvation and deliverance.

We know what physical salvation means. This obviously has to do with deliverance from circumstances that threaten our life or well-being. But spiritual salvation is an entirely different story. What does it mean to save our spirit or soul?

An absolute fact is that no man gets out of this life alive. This means we are finite beings. We are not in control of anything that happens in the afterlife. Where do we go when we die, and how do we get there? These questions go unanswered for many. Yet the Scripture does tell us that He, the Lord, has put eternity in men's hearts.

> Ecclesiastes 3:11 He has made everything appropriate in its time. He has also set eternity in their hearts. Yet, so that man will not find out the work which G-d has done from the beginning even to the end.

The Lord has given us a glimpse a hope or longing for the eternal things. The word eternity in Hebrew is "olam." Simply translated it means…

> *properly concealed, that is, the vanishing point; generally time out of mind (past or future), ever (-lasting, -more, of old), lasting, long (time), (of) old (time), perpetual, at any time, (beginning of the) world (+ without end).*

Why would He give us this eternal longing if there was no intent of fulfilling it? What would be the benefit to mankind if salvation was only in this physical world and not meant to be applied to our eternal life as well. So let's address these questions in a simple Biblical way to make some sense of it all.

Why we need salvation

The book of (Bereishit) Genesis, chapters one and two, deals with the creation of man and the Lord's call on his life. Man was to multiply, fill the earth, and subdue it.

Genesis 1:27-28 G-d created man in His own image, in the image of
G-d He created him; male and female He created them. G-d blessed
them; and G-d said to them, "Be fruitful and multiply, and fill the
earth, and subdue it; and rule over the fish of the sea and over the
birds of the sky and over every living thing that moves on the earth."

Simple enough task when you consider there were no obstacles in his path. No obstacles, that is, except for free will and the
serpent. Every school child knows the story. The Lord gave them
every tree to eat from except the tree that bore the fruit of the
knowledge of good and evil. Satan tempted them. They gave in
after they were warned that eating would result in death. They
now had first-hand experiential knowledge of good and evil. The
Hebrew word that is used in Genesis 3:22 is "ya-dah." It means
to have intercourse with information, to know it intimately.

Genesis 1:22 Then the LORD G-d said, "Behold, the man has become like one of Us, knowing good and evil"

A primitive root, to *know* **(properly to ascertain by seeing),**
used in a great variety of senses, figuratively, literally, euphemisti-
cally and inferentially (including *observation, care, recognition*; and
causatively *instruction, designation, punishment,* etc.)

This means they now had experiential interaction with the
information the Lord had given them. Before they committed the
act of disobeying the Lord, they had mental assent to the
knowledge of sin, but they did not have first-hand knowledge of
sin. After they sinned they were no longer just observers of good
and evil; they had a relationship with it. This is what caused their
expulsion from the Garden of Eden. This is the origin of the
Lord's judgment for sin, which was death. Man and woman were
now imperfect—they disobeyed the Lord, and they sinned. The

Lord cannot have imperfection in His presence. They were now separated from the Lord.

In the Brit Hadashah (New Testament) book of Romans 3:23, we read that "all have sinned and fall short of the glory of the Lord." The penalty for this is found in Romans 6:23. "For the wages of sin is death." We need to see that sin is not the act that we commit; it is a state of comparison between the Lord and us. As a result of our compromised sinful state, we commit acts of sin. It is the fruit of our imperfect human nature. The Lord is perfect, but we are not; therefore, we fall short of His glory. The end result is separation from the Lord eternally. This is called the second death, as stated in Revelation 20:11-15:

> Then I saw a great white throne and Him who sat upon it, from whose presence earth and heaven fled away, and no place was found for them. And I saw the dead, the great and the small, standing before the throne, and books were opened; and another book was opened, which is the book of life; and the dead were judged from the things which were written in the books, according to their deeds. And the sea gave up the dead which were in it, and death and Hades gave up the dead which were in them; and they were judged, every one *of* them according to their deeds. **Then death and Hades were thrown into the lake of fire. This is the second death, the lake of fire. And if anyone"s name was not found written in the book of life, he was thrown into the lake of fire.**

Every creature gives birth after its own kind. Genesis 1:21 and 24 states: "G-d created the great sea monsters and every living creature that moves, with which the waters swarmed after their kind, and every winged bird after its kind;

> Then G-d said, "Let the earth bring forth living creatures after their kind: cattle and creeping things and beasts of the earth after their kind".

This is also the case with man. A now imperfect man gives birth to the same. I have raised five children. I presently have five grandchildren. I have observed that if you give a baby a chance to grow up in the best environment, there will still come a day when that child will lift up his or her hand to strike if you take their toy away or anger them in some way. I know I didn't teach my children to hit people. Who is the culprit? It is built into their imperfect nature.

Are we hopelessly separated from our Lord?

This is the problem: We are separated because the Lord is perfect and we are imperfect. As I said above, He is unable to tolerate sin in His presence, and we are unable to comprehend all that He is in His perfection. We need help to come before Him. The Lord loves us and has provided a way for us to be restored back to the fellowship we had with him when we were in the Garden of Eden.

Allow me to share with you a little analogy that I have used in the past at my congregation. If you wanted to go to the sun, the only way that could be achieved would be in a rocket ship that would resist the fury of the sun. It would also have to protect you inside from the heat. It would have to cover you in protection against the glory, power, and heat of the sun. Scientists say that our sun is a midget in comparison to the other stars that are in the universe. We can't even tolerate the power of one of the smaller suns in the universe; yet we think we can go before the Creator of the universe? If that is not audacity, I don't know what is.

Again, here lies the problem. Not only can't the Lord have imperfection in His presence, we are unable to tolerate His perfection. The Lord transcends time, space, and matter. He is not held back by any of the restraints of His creation. Even His heaven cannot contain Him. All things were created for our benefit. It's not like the Lord needed a place to live. Man is unable to comprehend these eternal concepts. They are supra-logical; above logic. Yet, in spite of all of this, He loves mankind and wants a relationship with fallible, volitional beings. So how can we come before Him?

The way home.

By way of the analogy used above, the Lord sent Yeshua to pick us up, like the space ship, and bring us before His glory. By the mere fact that Yeshua was the only one who was able to keep the Torah in complete perfection, He is the one who can come before the Father and comprehend His Glory. He was the one who was in the beginning with the Father in creation, as stated in the book of John, chapter one.

> In the beginning was the Word, and the Word was with G-d, and the Word was G-d. He was in the beginning with G-d. All things came into being through Him, and apart from Him nothing came into being that has come into being.

He was the one who fulfilled all of the prophecies. He was the one who was raised from the dead. He was the one who made a relationship with the Father available to the Gentiles, extending salvation to the entire world, not just limiting it to the Jews.

He is the one who shed His blood as the final sacrifice for the salvation of mankind. Every blood sacrifice that went before Him was a prototype and foreshadow of the one to come and bring atonement to humanity. The sacrifice of the blood of the spotless lamb was the covering over our sins. This covering was called a kapparah. This is the root word we use to get the term Yom Kippur, the Day of Atonement, or more literally, the day of covering.

Yeshua, our "space ship," as strong and perfect as the Father, brings us to the Father because we are covered and protected from His glory. We can now be brought before the Lord's perfection because of the Kapparah, atonement—the covering of the blood.

Salvation in this case means being brought before the presence of the glorious Father, the creator of all creation, and being restored in right relationship with Him. This is something we cannot do on our own. This had to be done for us on our behalf. We have no power on our own to affect the eternal realm. This is where grace comes in. Grace is receiving something we don't deserve. We certainly did not deserve salvation. But because of the Father's love for us, we are blessed with the gift of eternal life. All we need to do is get on board the spaceship, figuratively speaking, so that we could be brought before the presence of the Lord.

During the first Passover, the children of Israel had to have faith in the blood of the lamb in order to be saved from the Angel of Death. Now we accept the blood atonement of the spotless Lamb to escape death. This time it is not physical death we are escaping—it is spiritual death and eternal separation from the Lord. Who needs salvation? Everyone! Whom did the Lord choose/create to bring this salvation to the world? The Jew! How was it fulfilled? Through the Messiah of Israel through His atoning sacrifice. He was the final sacrifice, described in Isaiah 53.

So if you haven't done so yet, get onboard the ship, and find covering and atonement in the only One who can affect your eternal salvation. Accept His grace and salvation, so you too may be restored and live eternally in His presence. This is the purpose of your creation.

We read in Romans 10:

> ....that if you confess with your mouth Yeshua *as* Lord, and believe in your heart that G-d raised Him from the dead, you will be saved; for with the heart a person believes, resulting in righteousness, and with the mouth he confesses, resulting in salvation. For the Scripture says, "Whoever believes in Him will not be disappointed." For there is no distinction between Jew and Greek; for the same Lord is Lord of all, abounding in riches for all who call on Him; for "Whoever will call on the name of the Lord will be saved."

Let"s wrap it up already.

With all that has been said, how do we wrap up this part of the book without being redundant? If there is any point that deserves repeating, I would say that we are a family that the Lord has established to reconcile the entire world back to Himself starting with Abraham. This is the essential message of the Gospel. The Lord created His family for the purpose of bringing the Messiah to the world. He welcomed all mankind to join this family. He even went as far as to give everyone a written invitation—His Word. The tempting and accusing angel, Satan, has done all that he could to keep the world from entering into the blessings of relationship with the Father through the Son. But I know that G-d still wins in the end. I cheated; I read the end of His book!

All believers in the G-d of Abraham, Isaac, and Jacob, should be tenacious in their defense of the faith. They can do this effectively only by knowing and understanding the family into which they have been adopted, and accepting the full blessing of their adoption.

Welcome to the family.

Chapter 13:
My Testimony

I really labored with the issue of how long I wanted to make this work and then how to end it. After much prayer I decided to do something that at first went against my better judgment. I don't want this book to be about me. I want the attention to be on the Word and the Messiah of Israel and the world, Yeshua. So even though ending it this way is very difficult for me, I would like to share with you my personal testimony. Please understand it is not because I feel that you need to hear my story, but because you need to hear my journey, and how the Lord can reach the Jewish people with the message that Yeshua is the most Jewish person a Jew could meet. That being said, this is my journey.

A wandering Jew comes home.

I was born and raised in the city of Boston, MA, in a section of Boston that was called Mattapan. When you entered my community, a sign said, "Welcome to Mattapan, a Suburb of Boston." That was not totally correct. The days of Mattapan's glory were definitely in the past. To say it was a suburb was like declaring "da Bronx" a suburb of Manhattan.

Nonetheless, in its time, Mattapan and the surrounding communities of Dorchester and Roxbury were some of the most densely Jewish populated areas in the U.S. I heard that it was second only to New York City. That being said, it was still a very large Jewish community, even when I was a youth.

I went to an Orthodox Synagogue, but we were, more or less, "conservadox." That meant we went to an Orthodox Synagogue, but we drove on the Shabbat to a place where the Rabbi couldn't see us, and then we would walk the rest of the way. For those of you who are not familiar with this practice, Orthodox Jews don't drive on the Shabbat. This was our way of getting around this while still looking good to the community and the Rabbi. We weren't fooling anyone; they all knew.

I went to public school, and in the afternoons I went to Hebrew school. I don't know if this was because my parents wanted me to get a real Jewish education, or they just wanted to keep me out of their hair for as long as they could.

My father wasn't what you would call a religious man. He wasn't trained in Judaism as a youth, even though his father, a Jewish immigrant from the Ukraine, was. I am sure he was trying as best as he could to do right by his children, and make sure that we got something he never did.

My brother, Joseph, was the real Jew in the family; he took his religious education very seriously. He had a beautiful voice, and aspired to be a Cantor. I, on the other hand, being the youngest of five and a total spaz, had problems in Hebrew school. It just didn't seem relevant to me and my ADHD way of life. I struggled all the way through. I did so poorly that my parents had to obtain private lessons for me so I could complete my studies and become a Bar Mitzvah (Son of the commandments). My teacher, the beloved but very aged Mrs. Lom, guided me through with the patience of a saint. I have a sneaking suspicion she'd been through the routine a couple of times before.

In spite of the large population of Jews, Mattapan was still a very mixed community. One of the larger groups was the Catholics. As a matter of fact, our next door neighbors were Catholic. Their daughter was my first friend. Her name was Veronica. She really was a good buddy to me for the first nine years of my life. But in spite of that friendship, my mother warned me to keep my distance from them. I remember one day when we were playing, I took the name of "Jesus" (Yeshua) in vain, and Veronica told me, in no uncertain terms, that the only fate for those who took the name of "Jesus" in vain was purgatory. Well, this was news to me. What was this purgatory that I was destined to go to, and who was this "Jesus?" The only thing I knew about this name was that my parents used it to curse, and His middle initial was H. Of course when I consulted my mother, she told me with all authority that He was the first Catholic and that I needed to keep my distance. This was my introduction to "Jesus".

We lived in Mattapan until I was nine years old. The demographic of our community was changing drastically, and as in many other places, the Jews made their exodus and other people moved in. We moved to the city of Brockton, MA, the home of Rocky Marciano, and the shoe capital of the world during World War II. There were a number of Jews who made their exodus to this city, and as a result, there were four synagogues to choose from. My folks, of course, chose the Orthodox one, and our life continued as "conservadox" Jews. My brother did well and merged right in with the Jewish life he always knew. I didn't do quite as well.

I was a very troubled young man, and I had a difficult time finding my way in the world. I was like Reb Suanders', son Daniel, in Chiam Potack's, The Chosen. I aspired to the worldly life. My taste buds were wet primarily because of the Ed Sullivan Show.

I remember as a youth watching the acrobats on the show flipping, juggling, riding unicycles, and doing all manner of comedy and "schtick". I couldn't get this out of my head. I thought to myself, if I couldn't be one of the Beatles, then I would be an acrobat and comedian. Jerry Lewis was my hero. If I could only be as funny as Jerry Lewis and flip as well, OY! Would I have it made! After all, he was Jewish and got away with it. Why couldn't I? My fate was decided then; I would be a Jewish funny flipper.

I started taking lessons at Shirley Matta's School of Dance in Brockton, MA. It was okay, though, because I stayed away from the dance part and took basic acrobatics from a private teacher. I was on my way to fame and fortune. I really excelled as an aspiring young acrobat; I took to it like a gefilte fish in jellied broth. I remember when I had my first recital—I was the star of the show. I did all manner of back bends, cart wheels, and head stands.

When I turned thirteen, as I prepared to be Bar Mitzvah, I remember that my father would drive me to Mattapan from Brockton so I could complete my private lessons from Mrs. Lom. We were going to the Synagogue in Brockton, but they wouldn't let me have my Bar Mitzvah there because we were unable to come up with the money to rent the hall. My father had been hurt in a job-related accident and was disabled. So our old synagogue in Mattapan said we were welcome to have my Bar Mitzvah there. I will have to admit that this really left a bad taste in my mouth concerning any further religious pursuits in my life.

I had a small event because of my father's disability. We were just unable to afford the kind of Bar Mitzvah that my brothers had. I didn't really feel gypped though, because I understood my father's predicament. I can say, however, that the synagogue and all that they taught me felt so distant to real life. I can't tell you that I really remember a lot that went on then. I don't ever remember being taught anything about the Scripture. The only thing that really stuck with me was Mrs. Lom, the loving way in which she taught me, her tremendous patience for a spaz like me, and how she taught me my Bar Mitzvah liturgy.

There are two sections to a Bar Mitzvah: The Torah portion, and the Haftorah portion. The Torah is the Scripture passage from the Five Books of Moses (Chumash), and the Haftorah is from one of the Prophetic Books. Part of my Haftorah passage was from Zechariah 2:10-11

> "Sing for joy and be glad, O daughter of Zion; for behold I am coming and I will dwell in your midst," declares the LORD. "Many nations will join themselves to the LORD in that day and will become My people. Then I will dwell in your midst, and you will know that the LORD of hosts has sent Me to you."

When I became a Messianic Jew, this verse became very significant to me. It was almost like the Lord was speaking to me early on, with a verse that would touch me concerning my future. I believe that G-d's plan for my future was carved out from my beginning. He knew I would eventually respond to Him, and He paved the road of my life very specifically, and spread out bread crumbs for me to pick up at strategic times.

After my Bar Mitzvah, I backslid from Judaism and became an aspiring young hippy and gymnast. Believe me! I know how ridiculous this sounds. My life was a real bag of contradictions. As a matter of fact, I was trying to become a hippy just as that fad was moving out of vogue and disco was moving in. The hippies just seemed so much more philosophical than the disco crowd.

Well either way, I did my best to replicate that lifestyle, even though I was a day late and a dollar short. Included in that lifestyle were the drugs, partying, alcohol, eastern mysticism, and anything else we could get away with. We even tried our hand at streaking for a while. Not a pretty mental picture, sorry.

All the time I was living this lifestyle, believe it or not, I was developing my skill as a competitive gymnast and doing very well. I won a number of very important meets and in my senior year took third place in the State of Massachusetts on floor exercise; I missed second by a fraction of a point.

By the end of my high school career, I had gotten into a lot of trouble and escaped most of the penalties that I should have received. I was doing drugs with my teachers and feeling like quite the big shot. But I was not happy at all. I was so out of control that, when I turned 17, I took off and hitchhiked to Canada just so I could meet up with a girl that I had met in Old Orchard Beach, Maine, so we could party. I didn't tell anyone where I was. My mother almost had a nervous breakdown because of my actions. They put out an all-points bulletin on me from Maine to Florida. You would not have wanted me as your kid, trust me.

It is rather funny though, the entire time I was living in this rebellious lifestyle, G-d was very faithful to bring many people into my life who would share with me the love of the Messiah, in a very loving and sensitive way.

One of those folks was a young man I met at Boy Scout camp on Cape Cod. I wish I could remember his name. I was 16 years old and he was 18. I presented a real problem to the camp. I was a camp counselor that summer. During the week we would do our job and on the weekends, when the boys would go home, we would go to the beach on Saturday night and get drunk while wearing our scout uniforms. It was a very disturbing picture seeing Boy Scouts drunk on the beach like little drunken sailors. On Sunday mornings we would get up receive another crew of boys and do the Boy Scout thing all over again.

This young man would spend time with me during the week and ask me questions about my faith and my life. He never pressured me, but he always challenged me. He was a strong believer and real gentleman. He had a calling on his life and, if I remember correctly, I think he was going to study for the ministry after high school.

It was the last day of camp and he asked me to come to his cabin because he had a present for me. This, I thought, was too cool to be true. He liked me enough to give me a present. I went to his cabin and he presented to me a very finely wrapped box. With great excitement I opened it, only to find that in the box was a Bible with the New Testament. This was definitely not what I was expecting. I thought to myself, "What the blank was I going to do with a Bible?" I received it with the appropriate grace and proceeded to plan a way to get rid of this "Christian" book.

I ended up taking the Bible home with me and I threw it out in the garbage. I felt so guilty that, in less than a day, I pulled it out of the garbage and put it in my underwear drawer. Surely no one was going to find it there. The Bible made its way around my room for over two years. But G-d had another plan for His Word.

It was the end of my senior year in high school. I was an aspiring BMOC—big man on campus. My gymnastic career was really taking off, and I was in a place where I was poised to win a state title. I had friends and the partying was at a frenzied pace. I was finally coming into my own. The only problem was I was failing in school, out of touch with my family, and out of control.

In the middle of my senior year, my parents hit me with a bombshell. I was told they were selling the house I had lived in for the last nine years, and they were moving to Albuquerque, New Mexico. I had never even heard of Albuquerque before, except in a Bugs Bunny cartoon.

Well, this wasn't going to do for me. I had no intention of leaving in the middle of my senior year in high school to either have to repeat it or finish it somewhere else. They wanted to take their sweet time and drive across country at their leisure, until they found a city to settle in out west, in or near Albuquerque. They couldn't wait six months until I finished school. I told them I wasn't going with them; they told me to find a friend to live with. That's what I did. I moved in with my friend Vinal and his family.

Vinal was a good kid. His family was pretty normal, as far as that goes. His mother and grandmother were strong believers. All Vinal needed was someone like me to move in with him and influence him in the wrong way. That's what I did. I introduced Vinal to drugs, partying, eastern mysticism, and all manner of debauchery. His mother, on the other hand, introduced me to a side of Jesus (Yeshua) that I had never known before. I guess G-d was trying to even up the score a little on Vinal's behalf.

As my life grew wilder, the Lord's work in my life took on more of an active influence. I remember the time when Vinal's grandmother, Nana, told me that transcendental meditation was from the devil. When we were alone, Vinal and I laughed out loud about that statement. Vinal's father was a rather distant fellow, but a good-old boy. He did have some very strong feelings about certain minorities, and I think mine was one was of them.

The difference this time with these "Christians" was that they took me in and didn't beat me up. I remember seeing Vinal's mother reading her Bible. This was definitely a new phenomenon to me. We certainly never cracked open a Bible in my house. This piqued my curiosity, big time.

My stay at Vinal's, though only six months or so, was a tremendous eye opener to me. I saw loving people who called themselves "Christians" and tried their best to live it out in their actions. Vinal's father eventually came to the Lord later on, and I was now faced with the same question I had to deal with before: Who the heck was this Jesus?

Unfortunately, Vinal's mom only had so much control over me; after all, I was not her kid, and I was only staying with them for short while, as well as the fact that I did pay them some rent. So my life was very out of control even under their auspices.

I was having the time of my life, but I was miserable from every pore of my body. I remember going to a party at my friend Bruce's house. You know; the kind of teen parties that you see only in the movies. The pot and alcohol flowed free like the water bubbler in school. I got so drunk and high, all I could do for the entire night was cry. Every time one of my friends would pass by the couch I was on, they would say, "He's still crying," and walk away. My life was a wreck, and I was too screwed up to know how bad I really was.

I graduated high school by the skin of my teeth and some bribery. I didn't stay in town long enough to walk the line at my graduation ceremony. My father drove back to Brockton to tie up some loose ends, and he picked me up a week before graduation. I remember the drive across country was very slow and painful. I was now ripped out of the only environment I knew. I missed my friends, my way of life, and my freedom, and I didn't trust my parents.

We finally made it to Albuquerque, and I was a wreck. I knew no one. So I turned to the only thing I knew how to do well for comfort—work out. I was out of control again, but this time I had no friends to party with, so I ran...and I ran, and I ran. I was like Forest Gump. I didn't know what to do with my life, so I just ran. I was doing ten or so miles a day. I also turned heavily to meditation for some solace.

My parents had sold their home in Brockton, and when they moved to New Mexico they bought a mobile home. They moved into a mobile home park very close to Sandia Air Force base. At that time, civilians could still get on the base relatively easily, and

I would just run past the check point booth, get into the base and explore. I ran all over that base.

After a month or so I met a young woman at the pool in the mobile home park. Her name was Carol and she was my age. She had also just graduated from high school, and lived with her aunt and uncle, Tom and Beth. Her uncle was a big, strong man. He walked with crutches; he had lost one leg as a child because of cancer. Tom accomplished more with one leg than most men would have with three. He also worked on the base. I never really knew what he did, although he did tell me that if I ever found out what he did, he would have to kill me. I believed him. Oh, did I mention he was also a Bible-believing, card-carrying, verse-quoting, born-again "Christian" This man knew his Bible, "Old Testament and New." I really liked Tom and Beth, they were genuine.

Unfortunately, their niece Carol was not serving G-d at the time and was looking to sow some wild oats. I just happened to be the first oat that she found, and I was still wild. We started a relationship, and let's just say that it did not honor G-d at all. She really was a lovely young woman inside and out, but as teens go, the streak of rebellion can run deep. Her uncle really took an interest in me, and he started sharing with me Biblical principles in ways that I had never heard before. I liked Tom a tremendous amount, and the things he taught me about G-d were real. They stuck to me like a good bowl of cream of wheat in the morning.

The Lord used that man in my life in spite of the sin I was in. He was the first "Christian" in my life that I ever took seriously. He didn't beat me over the head with a ten pound reference Bible, and he knew his stuff. I didn't come to the Lord at that time, but my interest in this "Jesus" character was definitely greater than ever before.

Toward the end of the summer, Carol was shuffled out to another aunt in California. I think Tom realized that I was not a good influence on her, and felt it was best to get her somewhere else. Yet, in spite of that, Tom did not revile or reject me. He was a true representation of the Lord's love and acceptance in my life. He was a "Christian" who didn't beat me up.

My high school gymnastic coach came out to see me that summer on his yearly trek across country. I thought he was the coolest thing on two feet. We smoked dope together in high school, he dated one of my best friends, and he lived in his converted van. How much cooler does it get than that? Basically, he was a druggy, sex offender with a teacher's degree. Today he would have been sent to jail. In the 70's, he was cool.

He was on his way to California, and when he stopped through, I decided to hitch a ride to the Rockies. Carol was gone, I was alone again, and it wasn't like my parents had anything to offer me. So off I went with my backpack and ex-coach into the sunset, in the coolest van this side of the Mississippi. The difference was that this time, in my backpack, I had the Bible that was given to me at Boy Scout camp two years earlier. The Lord wasn't done with me yet.

We drove north to Colorado, getting high the entire way. We made it as far as Estes Park, Colorado, and parted ways. He headed west, and I headed for the hills. My intention was to climb the Rockies and commune with nature. I started my ascent with a backpack, sleeping bag, my supplies, and a Bible.

When you climb a mountain you have a lot of time on your hands to think—and think I did. I took my time and enjoyed every minute of my trip, but I still found myself very discouraged and confused as to what I was doing and where I was going. I did not have any purpose for my life. I had lived it up with gusto. I had experienced many things in my short life of 18 years. But nothing that I did up to that point brought any real joy or fulfillment. I found myself becoming more despondent as I climbed the mountain and spent time alone. I actually found myself talking to the Lord and not even realizing it.

I remember that the only time I had ever really spoken to the Lord before this was when my father left my mother for a week, after a big fight, when we lived in Brockton. I was in junior high school. I prayed for a week for my father to come home. This was only the second time in my life—up until then—that I had ever really spoken to G-d.

Well, I made it to the top, and once I was there, I had no idea where to go from there. I was a young man on top of the world, with nowhere to go. This was the place in my life that I never wanted to be. This new status of being a real "nowhere man" forced me to confront the entire worth and purpose of my life. I wasn't happy, and nothing I had done up to that point ever brought me lasting happiness. What was I to do with my life? Where was I to go? What was my purpose?

It just seemed right that I should be there asking these questions. If there was a G-d in heaven, maybe He would hear my cry at the top of that mountain. I was closer to heaven after all. After what seemed to be an eternity of crying out to the Lord and struggling with the thoughts of just ending it all by jumping, I believe that G-d heard me and answered my cry. It was then that a voice went through my head, and it said: "Read that Bible!" I had been unable to throw it out and, believe me, I had tried a number of times. I decided instead to put it in my backpack. I carried it around while I traveled but never read it until that moment. Needless to say, I didn't jump; but I did finally pull that Bible out of my backpack.

I ended up so engrossed in reading it, that I read the entire New Covenant from beginning to the end. As I read, I started to understand that this Jesus (Yeshua) wasn't Catholic or Protestant. He wasn't even a "Christian," as a matter of fact; He was a Jew, and a Rabbi at that! Who would have thunk it—Jesus a Jew! Well, this had to be investigated. I had been wrongly taught, and now I wanted to know the truth.

Through that episode, I did finally come to faith. Don't ask me the day or hour; I don't know when. I didn't even know how to say a sinner's prayer. No one ever taught me to speak in King James English either. All I know is that "faith comes by hearing, and hearing the Word of G-d" (Romans. 10:17). When I finally came down from that mountain, all I wanted to do was tell people about Yeshua. My homily went something like this: "Hey man, Jesus is the Messiah; you need to check out this Bible, it's cool. Hey, did you know He was Jewish?" Obviously, my preaching skills still needed some work.

From that point on, I was the proverbial "bull in the china shop." Everyone needed to know this Jesus (Yeshua). My life now had purpose. I was to love the Lord and spread His word. Where to go from here? I didn't know, and I didn't care. G-d was in charge, and that's all that mattered. I was a homeless, fuzzy little Jew on a mission. I felt like one of the first disciples.

It was after I came to faith that life really started to get interesting. Never in my life did I meet so many religious whackos. It seemed as if the flood gates of hell itself opened up to make sure I didn't remain on the right path. The Lord was faithful to keep me and make sure I didn't fall into the hands of any nefarious characters or false prophets, although there were some very close calls.

After a very long trip around the western half of the country, a lot of close calls, and some divine appointments, I found myself back in Albuquerque. It was late at night, around 3:00 a.m., and I was sitting at a Winchel's Donut Shop on the corner of Central and Wyoming Boulevard. I was down to my last few cents. I had enough money to buy a coffee and a donut, and life was still good. I pulled out my Bible, well worn by now, and I started to read and enjoy my indulgence in my coffee and sugary delight.

My parent's mobile home was only about a quarter of a mile away. As I read, I asked the Lord for direction as to what I should do. What I really wanted to do was to once again put out my thumb and hitchhike back east to the Boston area to visit and witness to all my friends. After a long time in prayer and reading, I felt impressed to go home to my parents and share with them my new-found faith in the Messiah of Israel.

I finished my donut, put on my backpack, and walked to their house. It was too late to wake them up, so I just slept on the porch. As was my father's custom, he would walk their little schnauzer—that rat of a dog—every morning around 7:00 a.m. I remember being woken to the sound of the door on the porch opening and the schnauzer barking. As my father opened the door, he was startled by the sight of a body in a sleeping bag on his porch. The rat dog wasn't; he smelled me a mile away. I poked my head out from the bag and heard my father exclaim, "My son, the bum, he's home! So, what have you learned all these months you've been gone, my son, the bum?" I looked up at him from my sleeping bag, still a little groggy from lack of sleep, and said without dropping a beat: "Gee dad, I found Jesus as my personal Lord and Savior." My father ran promptly into the house yelling for my mother. "Sophie, your son, the bum, is home, and OY! You don't want to know from this!" Life from that point on, as bad as it was before with my parents, just sank to an all-time low. It was after that little episode that my father stopped speaking to me for a long period of time.

For the sake of time and space, let me just say that G-d was very gracious to me and made sure that I got involved in a very solid Bible-preaching church. I ended up at Central Assembly of G-d on Central and Zuni. The church was right around the corner from my parents' home. It was the same church that my good brother, Thomas Heine, went to. There he introduced me to two men who would be, until then, the most influential people in my life.

Gerald B. Manning was the pastor of that church. Pastor Manning not only led that congregation, but he was also an executive for the Sears Corporation in Albuquerque. He also owned a farm in Fredonia, Kansas, where he was from. He was a very imposing, yet loving man. He took real interest in the personal discipleship of the young men in the congregation. I was no exception.

Pastor Manning would always come up to me and say, "Henry, Henry, my little Jew boy, you're a seed of Abraham. Someday you're going to be a rabbi, Henry." Every time he would say that, I would choke up and beg G-d, "Please, anything but a rabbi." I wanted to be a preacher, not a rabbi. I believe that Pastor Manning was prophesying over me and didn't even know it, for this is what I became years later.

Even though Pastor Manning didn't know the Gospel from its Jewish context, he loved the Lord and his congregation with an unquenchable passion. He saw the call on my life and invested in me. He was the kind of man and pastor that every young person needs in their life. He used his calling in life to facilitate the calling of others (2 Timothy 2:2). He was my Rav Shaul. I think of him often and miss him profoundly.

The second man the Lord brought into my life was my youth pastor, Windell Splawn. Windell was a big white Texan, with such a thick accent, that every time he spoke, grits would cook themselves. I was still very rough around the edges at that time, and Windell was just what the doctor ordered to keep me under control. Windell was single, and was like the big brother that I needed but never asked for.

He was another one who saw G-d's call on my life. He was convinced it was his job to civilize me. I still had a "wandering Jew" roaming around in my system, and it was very hard to keep me from just taking off. Windell went so far as to invite me to move in with him so I would have a place to live. At that time I was living in a 1959 GMC van. The rent was cheap and the landlord was very forgiving. I was still in need of some cultiva-

The Lord Chose... Who???

tion. When homelessness gets into your "kishkes" (guts), it takes some time to be set free of that mentality and way of life.

Windell was a very faithful servant, and he refused to let me go on my way. He discipled me, nurtured me, brothered me, and mothered me. I still keep in touch with him regularly. To this day he still invests in my life and ministry.

There were so many more people who invested in my life— too many to mention in this little book. I wrote about some of them to show you how far the Lord reached down to save just one person. These Gentile believers fulfilled their calling to provoke this little Jew to jealousy and, therefore, I have had the opportunity of fulfilling my calling.

That being said, it is my hope that this testimony of mine has been a catalyst for you to go out and inspire others. As the time of the Gentiles comes to an end and our Messiah prepares to return, I pray that the Lord will use you as a tool to bring His children, the sons of Abraham, back to Him, so that they might soon say, "Blessed is he who comes in the name of the Lord - Baruch Habah b'shem Adonai."

> Isaiah 49:22-23 Thus says the Lord G-D, "Behold, I will lift up My hand to the nations and set up My standard to the peoples; and they will bring your sons in their bosom, and your daughters will be carried on their shoulders. Kings will be your guardians, and their princesses your nurses. They will bow down to you with their faces to the earth and lick the dust of your feet; and you will know that I am the LORD; those who hopefully wait for Me will not be put to shame."

Since the first printing of this book, my father who passed on August 27th 2010 came to the Lord with a true confession of faith in Yeshua on his death bed. I was the one who witnessed this miraculous event. To this day I cry tears of gratitude every time I think of this.

Glossary of Terms In Alphabetical Order

Arminian: One who follows the teachings of the theologian Jacobus Arminias, (1560-1609). He was a Dutch reformed theologian who espoused the idea that human dignity requires an unimpaired freedom of the will.

Asherah or Ashtoreth: was the name of the chief female deity worshiped in ancient Syria, Phoenicia, and Canaan. The Phoenicians called her Astarte, the Assyrians worshiped her as Ishtar, and the Philistines had a temple of Asherah

Brit Hadasha: The Hebrew name for the New Covenant Scriptures.

Brit Milah: The covenant of the circumcision as commanded in Gen 17.

Calvinist: One who follows the teachings of the 16th century French reformer theologian John Calvin. He developed the five points of Calvinism. 1. Total depravity 2. Unconditional election 3. Limited atonement 4. Irresistible grace, 5. Perseverance of the saints.

Canaanite: The Canaanites were an ancient Semitic people who occupied the land of Canaan before the Israelite conquest

G-d: The custom of substituting the word "God" with G-d in English is based on the traditional practice in Jewish law of giving God's Hebrew name a high degree of respect and reverence. When written or printed, God's Hebrew name (and many other names used to refer to God) cannot be erased or destroyed.

Goyim: The nations, usually refers in the Scriptures to the Gentile nations.

Hadith: Hadith are regarded by traditional Islamic schools of jurisprudence as important tools for understanding the Quran and in matters of jurisprudence. It is also known as a saying of Muhammad.

Israel: This is the name given to Jacob after his encounter with the Angel of the Lord in Genesis 32:24-32. The name literally means the *Lord has striven*. The name given to the descendants of Jacob the inhabitants of the land promised to Abraham. The name of the Promised Land .

Midrash: Midrash is a form of rabbinic literature. There are two types of midrash: midrash aggada and midrash halakha. Midrash aggada can best be described as a form of storytelling that explores ethics and values in biblical texts. Midrash halakha focuses on Jewish law and practice. Midrash halakha attempts to take biblical texts that are either general or unclear and to clarify what they mean.
http://judaism.about.com/od/glossary/g/midrash.htm

Moadim: The Hebrew name for the appointed times and seasons found in Lev 23:

Moshiach or Mashiach: The Hebrew title for the Messiah. It means anointed

Rav Shaul: The Hebrew name of the Apostle Paul. Rav refers to his status as a rabbi.

Talmud: The Talmud is the oral law of the Jewish people consisting of two works. To simplify, the Mishna is a commentary on the Torah and the Gemara is a commentary on the Mishna. Another very small definition might be...The most significant collection of the Jewish oral tradition interpreting the Torah.

Tenach: An anachronim that means Torah, (the five books of Moses) Navim, (Prophets) V'Kitubim, (The writings). This is the name used to describe the entire writings of the 1st covenant.

Torah: The Torah is the Hebrew name for the first five books of Moses. The word literally means "Instruction", "Teaching".

Qur'an: The writings which are sacred to the Muslims.

Yeshua: The Hebrew name of the Messiah. His name means salvation.

About the Author

Henry M. Morse is an ordained Messianic Rabbi with a degree in Bible and Theology from Central Bible College in Springfield, MO. He has been in full-time ministry for over thirty-five years, serving as youth minister, evangelist, missionary, and congregational leader. Henry has ministered in over twenty countries and forty-five states. Currently, Henry lives in Stoughton, MA, with his wife Cherri, and has five children, six granddaughters, and two grandsons. He is the founding Rabbi of congregation Sha'ar Hashamayim in Stoughton, MA. He has served there for fifteen years growing this ministry from a living room to a full-scale outreach to one of the most densely Jewish populated areas in the US.

Henry was ordained a Messianic Rabbi by the congregation Kehilat She'ar Yashuv on December 30, 2000. This congregation is affiliated with Chosen People Ministries. Previous to that he was credentialed with the Assemblies of God and Jews for Jesus. He left both of these ministries in good standing. He was also the co-director for the national youth program for Chosen People Ministries alongside of Jay Bockish.

If you would like to have Rabbi Henry come and share with your congregation on the Jewish roots of the faith, please contact him at benafuchi@aol.com or by phone: **(508) 944-7393.** He asks only that the congregations take care of his expenses to get there and back up front and take a love offering for his ministry when he is there. Please feel free to check out another side of his ministry. His comedy CD features religious parody like nothing you have ever heard before. You can reach his site at, http://www.indieheaven.com/artist_main.php?id=7241